Forever *and* One Day

Deidre Robinson

BALBOA.
PRESS
A DIVISION OF HAY HOUSE

Scriptures taken from the Holy Bible, New International Version®, NIV®. Copyright © 1973, 1978, 1984, 2011 by Biblica, Inc.™ Used by permission of Zondervan. All rights reserved worldwide. www.zondervan.com The "NIV" and "New International Version" are trademarks registered in the United States Patent and Trademark Office by Biblica, Inc.™

Balboa Press books may be ordered through booksellers or by contacting:

Balboa Press
A Division of Hay House
1663 Liberty Drive
Bloomington, IN 47403
www.balboapress.com
1 (877) 407-4847

Because of the dynamic nature of the Internet, any web addresses or links contained in this book may have changed since publication and may no longer be valid. The views expressed in this work are solely those of the author and do not necessarily reflect the views of the publisher, and the publisher hereby disclaims any responsibility for them.

The author of this book does not dispense medical advice or prescribe the use of any technique as a form of treatment for physical, emotional, or medical problems without the advice of a physician, either directly or indirectly. The intent of the author is only to offer information of a general nature to help you in your quest for emotional and spiritual well-being. In the event you use any of the information in this book for yourself, which is your constitutional right, the author and the publisher assume no responsibility for your actions.

Any people depicted in stock imagery provided by Getty Images are models, and such images are being used for illustrative purposes only. Certain stock imagery © Getty Images.

Print information available on the last page.

ISBN: 978-1-9822-3264-1 (sc)
ISBN: 978-1-9822-3265-8 (hc)
ISBN: 978-1-9822-3266-5 (e)

Library of Congress Control Number: 2019911603

Balboa Press rev. date: 08/08/2019

Contents

To the memory of my grandmother, Frances Eileen Fisher Robinson, and in honor of my mother, Deborah Robinson. Without either of these women and their hard work and dedication, I wouldn't be able to be the strong woman I am today, and I would not have been able to finish this work without their valuable input on my life, my education, and my own spiritual journey. Although it has been many years since her passing, I still love my grandmother forever and one day.

Acknowledgments

I wish to profusely thank God, my family, my friends, and the people who have supported me through each draft of these writings. You helped make the writing process real and exciting again. Also, I'd like to thank the many friends and fellow emerging writers I've met along the way. Your invaluable help and friendship can never be quantified appropriately.

You cannot find peace by avoiding life.

—Virginia Woolf

Prologue

Be Still

Flying doesn't happen without momentum. You run. You use your powers of levitation to get a view of your neighborhood that only eagles, seagulls, and pigeons are privileged to see. Looking down on your neighborhood, everyone you know is living their lives. Bustling about from the corner store to their cars to head to work or some other mundane life task, they cannot see you. Inhaling steam-scented spray starch, you watch as people produce tickets in exchange for clean clothing. The scent wraps you in an ethereal embrace.

Your name is carried along with the blustery wind before a warm, familiar hand clasps yours. You don't know where you're headed, yet you are thankful for the company. Leading the way, you follow your grandmother as she guides you out of the neighborhood and toward the sun. Both of you enjoy a slow glide over the block until a swift-moving metallic noise heads in your direction.

A tether of rusty chains and manacles appears and clamps down on your grandmother's right ankle, forcing her to let go of your hand. Fingers grasping air, you watch as she is anchored to the only place you've known as home for these fifteen years of your life here on earth. A large metal anchor contains the main chain that connects your grandmother and your mother to the house. They've been chained from the right ankle of your grandmother to the wrists and neck of your mother. Their eyes are an exaggerated mix of resignation and hope as you notice the longest chain is between your mother and grandmother, and the shortest one is from your mother to the house.

"Fly, girl! Hurry!"

The yelled plea gets lost among the thundering heartbeat as your puzzled vision is blocked with those multiplying chains to claim their next captive. You start to fall. Your faith is lost. In desperate fear, you strain to fly away, but only a weak backstroke results.

The speed with which they attack and your paralyzing panic make you an easy target to be snared in your new looped and locked prison with your mother as a cellmate. With fiery eyes and a lion's roar, she explains that you can never leave her. You cry mute, yet defiant tears.

Subsequent dream sequences involve you breaking one of the chains in a slow dance with a yellow-plated scorpion bidding you to come closer and sample his poison. Sure, you could fly to the church or the post office, but you could never go too far from the neighborhood or your mother. The last time you have this dream, you manage to break the last chain. However, you cannot fly. You initiate a slow trot, which becomes a fast jog until you're praying the spirit of Flo-Jo inhabits you.

You run for your life. You bruise your heel. You get a cut over your right eyebrow. You have a gash on your left elbow from running. Velocity and momentum build like a locomotive trying to race a Corvette on fire.

Chapter 1

The Run-On

Mostly fearless. That's what you consider yourself. A relatively young woman, strong and independent and stubborn and outgoing and a little rude and even cocky at times. You once heard that perception is reality. The reality is that you're tired. Tired of the same old bullshit in the same old city with the same old tired-ass people.

When your grandmother transitioned to the elusive, and oft-speculated afterlife, you realize that there is no real purpose to staying in Philly. Despite working with the youth at the church, caring for your mother, Liz, with her constant appointments and general codependent neediness, and the history between you and Liz, you must move.

Trevor called you earlier this morning asking to meet in his office at the church. He didn't sound like his usual cheerful self, which raised some flags, but it's just because he's tired and doesn't get much help from the folks who claim they want the youth and young people in the church, but all they really want are people to boss around and give all the work to without any real contributions on their part beyond writing a check or appearing in those unforgiving wooden planks with cracks, dust, and numbers with years' worth of fraudulent grime and grit of racist, sexist, homophobic "holy" messages from another misguided haughty white Jesus follower/

leader. His insistence on looking at everything through the light of the Christian church and its religious edicts is something that you hold with mild disdain. With Trevor's middle initial being J, you want to know if it stood for John—but never enough to ask. He seemed to always be saying something or other about love being the way as if he were on a mount delivering a sermon even when speaking with the neighborhood and church youth in a safe space meant for artistic creativity.

It's your friendship with Trevor and sense of obligation that brought you out of your warm apartment on this brilliant, chilly winter Wednesday morning. Trevor, or Reverend Williams as you refer to him only in the presence of other church members, called you to work out plans for the end-of-year program that displays what the youth have been doing all year. You only joined the ranks of the youth group volunteers after an annoyingly mundane Christmas program. As an audience member and former youth group alum, you were not happy about what you watched. The adolescents hadn't bothered to study their lines, and you suspected it was because they weren't included on their Instasnaps or Facekiks or whatever the hell it was these millennials were into these days. *Do they even know English anymore?* No matter. You step out of your two-door Acura coupe, clicking the alarm three times for security—and to show off a bit. Life had been great as a consultant, especially because you never bother with the tithing situation. *Since when does God need money?*

Breathing deep and jagged, you walk the short yet wide, familiar crooked concrete path past the red swinging sign indicating that "All Are Welcome" in faded gold lettering attached to a rusted-out once upon a time black metal post in between two snow-covered bushes on your right. *Is that a hint of yellow?* Shaking your head, you search for the intercom labeled "Church Office" pressing the filthy off-white button. If you weren't craving a distraction from packing, you would've stayed in your Chestnut Hill apartment. *Why do I live somewhere where the wind hurts my face?*

You've got a million things to do, and you've only accomplished two of the thirty items on your to-do list before your trip to Chicago. Sighing with your usual impatience, you press the buzzer again, trying not to grumble aloud for fear of being heard on the intercom inside. *I should move to Chicago, but that's just another place where the wind would just disrespect my clothes.* Suppressing your normal profane tirades was something you're actively trying to clean up before people think you're really a retired navy seaman.

After waiting what had to be a minute, you press the buzzer again and then decide to try to handle. *Son of a bitch!* The door was unlocked, leaving you feeling like a penny waiting for change. Of course, Trevor would leave the door open like a hippie as if he wasn't aware of the fact that people have zero respect for churches anymore and that this isn't the City of Brotherly Love and Sisterly Affection as much as it's becoming every man for himself in this large urban façade of a city.

The large, red door closes behind you with an assist from the wind. You head up the two-four-six-seven steps to the second-floor office. The water fountain sputters to life in a futile attempt to cool the constantly tepid Schuylkill punch that passes for mostly lead-free tap water as you clutch the loosening-with-each-turn dull silver door handle to the auditorium that leads to the office entrance. Not bothering to see if anyone is downstairs before entering the always warm and dusty auditorium, you hightail it to the cozy, brightly lit office.

The church office boasts two desks and two doors. One door leads to a supply room, and the other to the pastor's study. Trevor has an indiscernible look on his face until he sees his old friend. His smile is more than friendly. "Hey, Savannah, how's everything been? I hear your business is doing well."

"Good Lord, Trevor! I didn't see you in there."

"Ha! You know I try to hide out back here whenever possible. I mean, I do tend to blend in with the paneling in here." Flashing a knowing smirk, Trevor keeps referring to the time a white parishioner

3

told him that he was so dark he blended in with the walls and that maybe he should open his eyes and smile sometimes.

"Oh, Lord. It's that kind of day already, huh? Reverend Williams, do you need a hug? Ha ha!"

"Ha! Stop that! You know I'm just plain ol' Trevor whenever we get together. No one else is in the building, Savannah."

"Oh, good." You take a beat to ignore the warmth between your thighs, especially after what happened before. "So I'll take two guesses as to how you found out that info."

"Now, you know I talked to your mom. She can't help but to brag about her only child." Trevor smiles as he grabs his ceramic white dove mug with his herbal tea, bringing it to his full lips as he sips, spying you mischievously. With a sudden jolt, he thunks the mug down, shakes his head, and leans back in his brand-new desk chair with lumbar support.

"Yeah, I know. It gets kind of annoying after a while. Sometimes, I feel like as soon as I tell her some shit, she goes bragging to anybody and everybody. Then folks wanna ask me questions like I wanna be bothered. Ain't nobody got time for that, for real, for real."

"So you Sweet Brown now, Savannah? You gonna have a song on YouTube? Cut it out!"

"Well, my last name is Brown."

"And you are sweet." Trevor leers with his half-cocked grin and raised eyebrow in your direction.

"Trevor …" you warn with faux disgust.

"I know. I shouldn't mention it. I'm sorry, Savannah."

You sigh with a heaviness you do not feel. "Trevor, we can't finish what happened that night, and you know why."

"I know, I know. But what am I supposed to do? I'm still a man, Savannah. I'm not perfect … if there is even such a thing."

Why does he have to look at me like that? "I know you're not. Neither am I. I know your wife and your kids. We got carried away, and it can't happen again."

4

"You're right." Stretching the taut muscles in his neck as he rounds his broad shoulders, he sneaks a peek at the picture of his wife and daughters on his oak desk and sighs softly.

"Look, we're here to talk about the kids. So what did you call me here for on this cold as fuck morning? And don't say to warm you up either."

"Ha!" Trevor chuckles and smirks as he takes a deep breath to focus. "Well, I called you here to see how you're enjoying working with the girls in the dance group. I know you were reluctant at first, but I'm hoping that the joy I see on your face is real."

"Of course it is. I love working with the girls and helping you keep everybody on task. All the older women do is sit, eat, and talk to each other in between yelling at the kids. Nobody needs that."

"True. I was also hoping that you'd consider taking over the youth group as its overall leader on a permanent basis."

"Uh … I'm sorry. What now?"

"Well, how about you take some time to think about it?"

"Trevor, why do I need to take over? You're the pastor, and that was the point of you coming here nine years ago. Are you tired of working with them already? I barely like adults let alone children."

"Well, I know I can trust you to not let the cat out of the bag, so I'll just tell you. Anna and I are looking for a new place to live."

"Say what? What do you mean?"

"Please don't be upset, but I'm tired of dealing with these people. They could care less about being active and caring church members or Christians for that matter. We're strongly considering moving back to Louisville."

"Wow. I knew things were crazy after I left a few years ago, but I didn't realize how tired you were to want to go back to Kansas City. How far has this 'strongly considering' gone? Do you have a job? Or a house? What about your daughter? What about Anna?"

"Actually, Anna has been having some issues at her job, which isn't even in her field. You know she's an art teacher, and finding a job—even as a substitute—has been hard in this school district. Even the private and charter schools are tough to get into."

"Yeah, that's true. I know she's been having issues. Has she found a job there already? Or are you still in the discussion process?"

"Anna has been down there for a second interview with an advertising firm that pays much better than where she is now."

"Whoa. A second interview? That's pretty serious." You've known it was bad, but not get the fuck out of Dodge bad. Then again …

"Yeah, Savannah. I've been in contact with the presbytery down in Kansas City, and there's a job they think I'd be a good fit for, but I'm not sure what I want to do yet."

"I think you're a great minister, and you're a great teacher as far as these kids and Bible study. Not that I've been to Bible study, but Mom really enjoys it when she makes it. And you know how she is. If you can keep her attention and make her think about a different interpretation, you've worked miracles."

"Yeah, true. I enjoy some of the members and certain activities, but it's just not enough. I'm tired, Savannah. I'm sick and tired of pretending like these not-so-subtle racist attacks don't bother me, and so is Anna. This place is fuckin' ridiculous! I've never been subjected to this shit as much in my life as when I moved to Philadelphia. *Philadelphia!* Really?"

"Trust me. I get it, Trevor. Just know that the Browns will miss you and your family." Someone is always leaving, it seems …"

"I know, Savannah. I'm sorry for yelling. I'm just frustrated that people think it's okay to talk to me and my wife the way they do. And I don't just mean church members either. My daughter sees the looks she gets when we all go out as a family."

"Damn." You pick up the photograph and study the six eyes frozen in faux happiness.

"She spends a lot of time in her room on Netflix or on social media, which I don't like, but what can I do? I can't protect her from everything." Trevor exhales, plunking back into the squeaky, black, torn leather chair, closing his eyes and contemplating how love could be met with such ugliness.

In the silence, you remember taunts of "white girl" at the hands of the other black kids at your private school. It wasn't your fault that you weren't allowed to speak slang or use profanity growing up, but you would rather be teased than deal with Liz's temper or soapy mouth cleansings. You shudder involuntarily before speaking. "Trevor, look …" You sigh as you choose precisely what you want to say. "If I could get out of this damn city, I would too. I'm only an auntie and not a parent, but I know that you can't shield your children from life's hurts and disappointments. All you can do is help them with the process and let them know that people's skewed views are theirs and theirs alone. Fuck 'em."

"You're right, Savannah. You always are. So you'll consider my question, right?"

"I don't know, Trevor. With Grandmom gone, I don't really have a reason to stay here. I need to give this some thought."

"Good. That's all I can ask for, Savannah." You're pleased to see some of the light returning to his mocha eyes.

"I guess I should go then. Unless you have something else you want to discuss?"

"Oh no. I'm going to go visit some of the sick and shut-ins for a couple of hours. Some of these deacons don't."

"Yeah, I've heard. You know, Mom is always telling me what's happening here whether I care to know or not." You share a healthy laugh together, which dissipates the tension. Because there's a sharing atmosphere, you decide to fill Trevor in. "I'm actually getting ready to go out of town for a while. For work."

"Really? Where are you headed?"

"Chicago. There's a client there who I'd like to visit since this is a new business relationship that I hope lasts for a long time."

"Okay! I see you, Savannah! Go do what you gotta do! Isn't your aunt out that way? Carole, right?"

7

"No. Aunt Carole moved to Florida. She retired and was going to move here, but with Grandmom transitioning, she decided to move somewhere warm. She spent thirty years out there with all that wind and cold-ass weather. She wants her retirement to be spent in warmth and comfort doing the activities she loves. She's very much the active sister."

Trevor had to giggle at that. "That is your mother you're talking about, Savannah."

"Yeah, I know. I love her, but she's so frustrating sometimes." You rise, grabbing your coat in preparation for the short, brisk trip to the car.

"You wouldn't have it any other way."

You flash a big grin, even showing some teeth, a rarity for you. You zip up your coat, secure your hat, and inhale deeply.

Trevor rises, coming from behind the desk to give you his customary hug.

You are careful to count three Mississippis in the standard platonic straight woman hug. It is bad enough Trevor still licks his lips with relished recall when they spend time together. *If there is a hell, I might be going. Could I have a pitcher of margaritas in my specially reserved section though?*

Not bothering to look back for fear he may be watching your hips in their rhythmic sway as you make your way to your ride, you begin recalling all the things you need to do before leaving. Your trip to Chicago isn't for another week in order to take Liz to previously scheduled appointments. Tomorrow is the eye doctor, and Monday will be the podiatrist.

Feeling the heft and smooth surface of your key fob, you push the unlock button as you exit the church and its stale, musty air. At a brisk pace, you lumber around the rear of your coupe and enter, calling the engine to life. Tuning to your favorite old school hip-hop and R&B station, you nod your head to "OPP" by Naughty by Nature and crank up the heat. You'd only been inside for about forty-five minutes, but the hawkish wind significantly cooled the car's interior. Good thing you opted against leather seats. Past vehicles either freezing or scorching your ass were the best lesson.

On automatic pilot, you navigate away from the crooked curbs and sidewalks of Shady Oak Presbyterian Church. Enjoying "Juicy" by Notorious B.I.G., you relax into the short fifteen-minute drive home. Deciding against stopping by your mother's, you still can't believe that the nineties were twenty years ago and wonder how that even happened. Wasn't it just yesterday that you were lamenting the deaths of Kurt Cobain, Tupac, and Biggie while remaining baffled at the whole East Coast-West Coast beef nonsense? And surely learning of Aaliyah's plane going down shortly after takeoff in the Bahamas and still grieving over the passing of her grandfather weren't fifteen years ago. There was still a timelessness about "If Your Girl Only Knew" "Player's Anthem" "Keep Ya Head Up," and "Smells Like Teen Spirit." "Just A Girl" by No Doubt certainly helps speed up your pace while exercising or walking just as "Reminisce" by Mary J. Blige causes you to break out into song almost wherever you are.

Yet, there are some songs that you skip just because the memories that accompany them were too much to handle. "Don't Leave Me" by Blackstreet, "You Are Not Alone" by Michael Jackson, "The One I Gave My Heart to" by Aaliyah, and "Desire" by En Vogue all are songs that are skipped in whatever music app or cause a change in radio station. Not that you don't love those songs, but the memories of long, sensual kisses, slow dances, and hearing your first love moaning your name flood your mind swiftly chased by the breakup phone call on Christmas Eve and wearing black for thirty days while contemplating joining eternity via a wrist-cutting suicide attempt in your family's bathroom induced sobs and self-loathing that hasn't disappeared over the twenty-year expanse of time.

Heaving your chest in an exaggerated breath that only the rearview mirror witnesses, you opt to adjust your focus back to your journey. Not that you want to go to the Windy Chi, but money beckoned, and you need a change of scenery even if only for five days. Maybe you could even see your favorite cousin. Maybe not.

She's made some interesting life choices that make you scratch your head. If pressed to speak, you don't think you could sustain silence. As much as you want to be in an honest and committed relationship, there is no way you can be like Leah and endure anyone who lacks drive, common sense, or even looks—no matter the history. Love, or the idea of it, makes people blind as fuck. You'll have none of that.

Chapter 2

Blind but Now?

Concluding a fitful sleep complete with hearing what you swear was your grandmother's voice calling your name, you set about the business of prepping mentally for your day with Liz. Liz can never just go to one place. After the eye appointment, Liz will undoubtedly want to find some food. Then, because she knows you can't possibly refuse your one and only mother, Liz will most likely ask if you two can go to the store and pick up a few things while she has the ride.

Liz's eye appointment is at ten, and it is nine fifteen. That's just enough time to grab the coffee that keeps America running, pick up Liz, and make the quick trip to the eye doctor. If you're going to endure your mother's nauseatingly chipper attitude, you need to have a major caffeine adjustment. Sneaking a glance at your emergency Newport encased in plexiglass on your living room desk, you travel to the double-locked door to exit. Your tolerance for your mother's strong suggestions dripping with extra sweet honey has been nearly nonexistent lately.

Once you exit the drive-through several minutes later with your steaming cup of good temperament, a cinnamon raisin bagel toasted with cream cheese, and a Boston cream doughnut for Liz, you make the familiar right out of the parking lot onto Chelten Avenue. Driving almost three blocks, your heart mimics arrhythmia at what you see. The street is blocked off, and traffic is being redirected.

There are cops galore, a fire engine, and an ambulance. A nearby row house is on fire. You hope it's not anyone you know. There are the usual people gawking with cell phones plastered to their ears with shower caps, slippers, and muffin tops hanging out for the world to see while watching the firefighters and policemen do their jobs.

After your brief forced detour, you pull in front of the house and take out your cell to dial the long-standing number. You know you should have the hands-free technology and stop being lazy. Before you can punch the last number, Liz emerges slowly with her purse and jacket and makes sure the door is locked. The small amount of patience you packed wanes at how slowly she walks down the stairs until it strikes you that Liz is taking her time because the sun is in her eyes. You take a deep breath and have some more of the medium French Vanilla coffee with cream and sugar while waiting for your favorite mother to open the passenger door.

"Good morning, Daughter! How are you this beautiful Thursday morning?" Liz's face beamed brightly.

"Good morning! I'm feeling pretty good this morning. How about you, Mom?"

"Blessed and highly favored."

"God, Mom. Is that your answer this early in the morning?"

"Of course it is, Niecy. If Jesus paid it all, then I can pay it forward with a positive attitude." Liz's smile is dripping with her usual too sweet flavor.

"Mom, one, don't call me that. I'm not a little girl anymore. Two, I don't think that's how that works."

"But, you'll always be Mommy's little girl—even if you don't like your cute little nickname."

"Mom, the nickname comes from my middle name, which I don't use. Ever."

"Well, someone's a bit snippy this morning. I'd ask you if you got your coffee yet, but I see you have some for yourself. Didn't bother to think about your mother this time, huh?"

"Actually, smarty-pants, I got you a doughnut, but no coffee because you won't drink anything until after your appointment is over like always." You swing the bag with the doughnut into Liz's chest, hoping your anger doesn't transfer to the motion of the bag.

"Oh, I spoke too soon. I'm sorry. What's with all the smoke?"

"There's a fire around the corner at one of those houses that are on the same block as the Fields' house, but it's not their house."

"Oh, okay. I hope nobody got hurt because that would be terrible." Your manner softens at that statement because it's genuine. Liz is a softy.

"There were using the cherry picker to go to the second-floor bedroom window, so I hope they got everyone out. Meanwhile, I need to go a different way to get to the doctor, so you won't be late."

"They blocked off the street?"

"Yeah, Mom. You can't have traffic and the K bus trying to get down the street. That would be a nightmare."

"True. That's probably the most action we've had around here in a long time. Well, aside from the ambulance coming to take one of the older neighbors to the hospital or the cops coming to get some of these young knuckleheads out here."

"True. It's just crazy nowadays. At least when I was growing up, the shady people had enough respect for life to not act crazy in front of old folks and little kids. These young-ass idiots could care less about anything."

"Yeah, it is, but enough about that. How are you, Savannah? Seriously."

"Mom, I'm fine. Why do you ask?"

"Can't a mother ask about her one and only daughter?" You shake your head at the often-asked question as Liz brushes crumbs off the family-inherited large breasts cloaked in a rouge-colored thick woolen coat from her Boston cream.

"Why, of course, you can, Mom. Can't I ask why you're asking? There's usually a reason for your inquiry."

"Why do you think I have to have a reason for everything? Seriously, Savannah, how are you?" Liz turned to give suffocating attention to her only child.

"I'm fine, Mommy." Willing a pleasant visage, you tighten your grip on the gray steering wheel and clench your teeth.

"Well, as your grandmother used to say, 'It's good to see your face.'"

"Um … thank you?"

"You're welcome, especially since you don't have time to spend with me besides my appointments these days." You roll your corneas with a smirk as you turn onto Old York Road, crossing Cheltenham Avenue into Montgomery County, the next-to-last turn before reaching the eye doctor.

"Mom, I spend plenty of time with you."

"Uh huh. I might have been born at night, but not last night."

"Okay … what do you want, Mom?" The pain in the knuckle of your right index finger alerts you to the death vise you've placed on the steering wheel, aggravating the old football injury. You release with caution.

"What's his name?"

"What's whose name? And why does it have to be a *he*?"

"Well, whoever it is who has my baby so wrapped up that she doesn't just pop up at my house to cook me dinner, that's who." Liz offered a "Mommy always knows" kind of Cheshire cat grin.

"Is this nerve-punching question session about dinner? Where are you going with this, Mom?"

"You know good and well that this isn't about dinner, Savannah. I don't see you as much. You've been distant lately. Daydreaming and mooning about when I do see you."

"Mom, I've just been busy. That's all." *Why does it seem so much longer to get to a stoplight in the suburbs?*

"You can, but I know that it ain't from Jesus and that coffee alone, so what's his name?"

"Mom, there's no one in my life right now. Honestly. And if there was, it doesn't necessarily mean a man, okay?"

"Are you sure? The last time I didn't see you for long stretches, there was that devil woman. What was her name again?"

"Mom, let's just not even bring her up this morning. Please."

"She still owes me my money, Savannah." Your gut flinches involuntarily.

"Yes, mother, I remember because you won't let me forget—ever."

Oozing with barely suppressed anger at that special brand of Mom-infused guilt, you turn the radio to a station you both enjoy. Luther Vandross's velvety crooning reminds you both that "A House Is Not a Home." A short exhale leaves your constricted chest cavity.

Liz gets the hint, and finally drops the subject, singing along to the songs she knows and asking about the stuff she doesn't as always. The best thing about listening to the old school R&B station is that you're both musically satisfied. Liz isn't aware of all your music from the nineties, but she does know the artists, most of the time, and that almost makes up for the prying grill session.

Almost.

As you arrive at the doctor's office, you pull up in front of the double doors, so Liz doesn't have to walk as far. It's not that she can't walk from a parking space to the door, but you still ensure that Liz can see well enough to get to where she needs to be in short distances. You rejoice at snagging a handicapped space, display Eileen's old handicapped placard, lock up the car, and go back to grab your phone from the cupholder. *Still no word from Trevor?*

You like that Dr. Johnson's office was always kind of quiet this time of morning, except for the occasional footsteps between the exam rooms in the back and the phone ringing. Walking through the designated office door in the large office building, you find your mother searching for you as one of the interns shifts their weight from one foot to the other with a plastered customer service grin.

Liz hands you her jacket and purse as she bounds behind the young, female intern as she leads her to the first exam room. Just

15

like Eileen, she always has a running conversation with anyone who provides a service. It didn't matter if it is a doctor, a nurse, or a medical assistant. Hell, it could be the maintenance worker, and she would strike up a conversation if she felt like it.

There is still so much to do before Chicago. You never like waiting until the last minute to get things together, especially when prepping to meet a client for the first time. Although it's a long train ride—you cannot bear the thought of flying in a man-made metal contraption during winter—you'd rather spend time enjoying window-seat views with a good book and assorted musical accompaniments.

After a half hour or so, there's still nothing from Trevor, but Liz emerges from the back all smiles behind Dr. Davis. He is smiling too, so Liz must've been following directions. For once. It stymies you why it is okay for parents to make their children follow doctor's orders, but then, once they reach a certain age, they no longer should. Or they decide to be their own personal physicians, as if that's okay. Liz is famous for skipping blood pressure or diabetic pills, but she uses those eye drops religiously. *So it's okay to see well but not to be able to move? I hope I'm not like that when I get that age. Sheesh!*

"Did you see both doctors that fast, Mom?"

"Yeah, right! You know I always have to wait for Dr. Johnson to get to the office, so he can give the all clear."

"Ugh. I was just hoping that you wouldn't have to have a ton of interns poking around in your eyes today."

"Yeah, I wish, but no. There were two interns in there with Dr. Davis, so they had to have a look to see how far I've come with my condition."

"Yeah, I know, but I'm sure you get tired of people digging around in your eyeballs. I know you have a rare condition, and thank goodness for Dr. Johnson, but it gets to be a bit much for you and me because I always have to wait for them to get done."

"Uh huh, but that's life. I'm just thankful that I can see as well as I can after the cornea transplant and the cataract surgeries. You know, I was able to see the sign-in screen all by myself today."

"Really? Well, that's great, Mom."

"Yes, ma'am! Ha! Thank you, Lord!"

"I'm glad. I don't want to be a seeing-eye dog like I was when I was a kid."

"I don't want you to have to either. I'm glad the days of wearing hard contact lenses and glasses are over. What ya working on, Daughter?"

"If you'll stop looking over my shoulder, Mom, I can tell you that I'm just finishing up my presentation for the marketing plan I've just completed for a company in Chicago. That's why I wanted to be sure you got to all of your appointments before I left."

"Well, thank God for that! You know, I love Michelle, but she can't drive worth a damn anymore. That's my buddy, but I can't see how she's still driving around when she's busting off side mirrors from people's parked cars."

"Or how she thought there was a dog in someone's front lawn when it was really a rock. That's not good. At all. Why doesn't her son help her out?"

"Because, between you and me, he ain't shit. Lord, forgive my mouth, but he's not."

"Well, I didn't want to say anything, but I saw him cursing his mother out like she was some random street person. Like, how is that okay?"

"It's not. I would've never even fixed my lips to speak to my mother the way he does."

"Neither would I. We don't always agree, but I wouldn't curse at you. That's just plain wrong."

"Sometimes, your grandmother and I would argue, but I've never called her out of her name."

"Sure, Mom."

"Well, I'll stop talking your ear off. I know you have a lot of work to do. I'll just read my Kindle. There's a juicy new Alex Cross book waiting for me to finish it."

You insert your earbuds before Liz starts yapping about her book obsession. Again. Pointedly, you ignore her stare that is imploring you to ask about this new book. You don't have time for that sort of thing. Recent events with Trevor and other lovers would make for a more interesting read.

At 11:04, according to Liz's Kindle, Dr. Johnson rushes in with rosy cheeks and a coat that is too light for the weather. He greets his staff and patients with his gleeful greeting before being sure to tell Liz that as soon as he got settled, she was up first. With Anita Baker singing about her "Sweet Love," you retreat into the presentation, which only needed two or three more slides before you are satisfied. Being a perfectionist when it comes to business is never an easy thing, but the benefits in your bank accounts ease the struggle for perfection.

About twenty minutes later, Liz taps you before going back with Dr. Johnson. *Finally.* Your eyes keep crossing, and you haven't made as much headway on the slides. You haven't heard from Trevor or anyone of any importance today. Trying to pretend that you don't have regrets about crossing that line, you try to distract yourself from any feelings. *Feelings are for the weak, and there's money to be made and a lifestyle to establish.*

Shutting down the laptop and cranking up Rihanna's "Cockiness," you feel the familiar urge to use the ladies' room, but you decide to wait for your mother. You'll probably both have to go anyway, and there is only one key. You take a deep breath and make a mental checklist of the things remaining to do before the trip, but your monkey mind wanders.

"Savannah, we need to talk."

"Um, okay." *I know I didn't miss any school phone calls because I didn't cut at all this week.*

"Would you care to explain this note to me?"

Holy fuck! The note from Diane. Shit! "Uh, what about it?"

"I was washing clothes, and it fell out your jeans pocket. What is this girl talking about, Savannah?"

Dammit! "Mom, it's not that big a deal. It was just a note."

"Really? It's just a note! Are you trying to tell me that you didn't allow some girl to do unspeakable things to my child? Is that what you're saying?"

"Um …"

"You'd better think long and hard about your answer, girl! Did you let some dyke touch you? Are you a dyke now? Am I raising some bulldagger in my own damn house?"

"Well, technically, it's Grandmom's house."

"Don't get cute, Savannah! Savannah Denise Brown, you'd better tell me right now. Are you a … dyke?"

I hate it when she gets all puffed up and starts balling her fists. "No, Mom. I'm not."

"Well, that's what I thought. I know I'm raising a good girl who would never do anything to disappoint me, right?"

"Yes, ma'am." *Don't cry. Just keep making eye contact.*

"Good. I know when we get to be teenagers, we get curious about things, but that is a path to hellfire and damnation! I want us all to be together in that great getting up morning when Jesus comes! Do you understand me?"

"Yeah, Mom."

"What?"

"Yes, Mom."

"Yes, Mom, what?"

"Yes, Mom, I understand, and it will never happen again."

"Good."

Let me get the hell out of this room.

"Oh, and Savannah?"

Shit. "Yes, Mom?"

"Look in the trash. I got rid of all those nasty books I found in your drawer while I was putting your clothes away. I bet that girl who keeps calling my house is giving you these books and all these demonic ideas, isn't it?"

I just want this conversation to be over.

"That's okay. You don't have to say anything. Just know that me and my house will only serve the Lord. You hear me, girl?"

"Uh, yes, ma'am."

"Now, go on and do your homework. We won't speak of this again, will we?"

"No, ma'am."

You dab at your eyes and pray no one in the waiting room sees your moment of vulnerability while you attempt to regain some semblance of calm. There is no way you'll be able to explain your changed visage. *This is no time for questions.* You skip past Marsha Ambrosius's "Far Away," and settle on an old Meek Mill "Dreamchasers" mixtape song instead. Hearing him rap with Beanie Siegel about chasing their dreams is better than the sad lyrics of Marsha about a gay friend of hers who'd committed suicide. You were almost that friend. Twice.

Just as Meek Mill ends the track with his signature line, "Chase ya dream, youngin'," Liz heads to the front counter. This is your normal cue to join her and help her set her next appointment. Liz doesn't have to come back for another six weeks. Her eyedrops will be reduced from three times a day to two. As Dr. Johnson is running down the reasons that Liz is his best patient, you manage a meek smile, struggling to remain in the moment.

Liz walks with you to the car instead of waiting for you to park in front of the outer office doors. It's not until you reach for the handle that you notice a small slip of crinkled pink paper stuffed there. Checking for onlookers, you toss it underhand into the grass in front of the car. It was probably someone selling something because there isn't any damage to the vehicle. It's not a ticket for parking in a handicapped space. You already know the Lord. You have a political party affiliation. You've purchased Girl Scout cookies, so there is nothing you're interested in reading on a flyer. Noting the time, you cruise out of the parking lot toward a nearby eatery. It is much easier to maintain stability when you're not hangry.

Chapter 3

She Fades (Le Chapître Noir)

The plops reminds you that global warming is a thing. With temperatures hovering in the forties and white, crystallized precipitation slinking into corner grates, you're thankful for clear paths as you emerge above ground from the L stop at Thirtieth and Market Streets and cross to the Amtrak station. With Liz's appointments done for at least nine weeks, you linger outside of the entrance and inhale the air of newness you imagine lies ahead. Habit forces you to shove your hands in your pockets in search of a Newport. Finding none, you sigh at the hint of steam wafting from the lopsided, pockmarked cement, you nod your head to an unasked question before entering the tall, archaic structure.

With its large cement columns, nineteenth-century molding with golden trim, and brilliant clocks, the Thirtieth Street Station is a fraction of New York's Grand Central Station, yet it feels the same as your destination. A part of you wishes you had business in New York City, but the twenty-seven-hour train ride will be a good time to review your presentation and relax.

Rushing to the train, which departs in twenty minutes, you avoid a collision with a passerby who reeks of piss, alcohol, and regret. Fashioned in multiple filthy, damp layers of clothing accompanied by one brown shoe and one black running over to the left sneaker that is beginning to lose the N emblazoned on its side, one of the city's many homeless attempts in vain to blend in with the travelers. Merged with sadness and fear, a shudder trembles through you at this man with his scraggy black and gray beard and hair.

He looks like the man who always rides the subway just after rush hour and hopes his long soliloquy will lead to money in his large fast-food cup. He rides the Orange Line between Erie and Walnut-Locust, occasionally using the free interchange at City Hall to board the L at Fifteenth Street, riding westbound until the last stop at Sixty-Ninth Street, where he begs in the station until the transit police convince him to walk the streets or board a train back to his main location at City Hall.

Unsteady energy pounces your frame, nerve by nerve, as Amtrak police and the Department of Homeland Security come to grab this silenced and saddened being. Your eyes connect in a brief flash of a helpless plea and guilt in an emotional call-and-response between humans. Scratching your eyes in a futile attempt to disconnect, you place your suitcase on the overhead rack and settle in your seat. As a child, you adored window seats.

The bleak cemented view begins to change as the train leaves the station. Passengers are still settling in as you debate which playlist you'll listen to. Switching from hip-hop to R&B to jazz leaves you with a dissatisfied taste in your mouth and causes you to sigh with an audible echo. At times like these, you find some classical music to help sort out your thoughts. And after the dream you had the night before, you know that your wandering mind has only gotten started with the torture. Checking your phone for a phantom text, you pretend that disappointment and gloom aren't settling into your brow.

The song forever associated with the Dance of the Sugar Plum Fairy from Tchaikovsky's "The Nutcracker Suite, Op. 71a" provides the soundtrack to a brief smile session reflected from the window back to you amid the trek through dilapidated buildings, bald truck tires, and naked trees. You remember how proud Grandmom was when she talked about Mom being in a production of *The Nutcracker* as a young girl. Her darkened sea salt-caramel face framed in thinned, wavy silver and black hair opened as she spoke of her firstborn. Mom even performed some of the choreography as she remembered. Three generations of Brown women engaging in laughter while reminiscing about whatever came up in conversation. Such is love.

A face full of light and love is how you struggle to remember Grandmom, not the memories that plague you on those nights you tussle between nightmares and insomnia. Inky black nights where your spirit and ego clash in mortal combat. On nights where hurt and pain scream, "Finish her!" as your spirit insists on claiming a flawless victory, the copious amounts of THC inhaled only serve to trigger what must be faced.

Miniature eyes vibrate each nerve ending like a requiem for love. A requiem for life. A requiem for the grandmother. Her mute physicality decaying the heart space in loved ones whose disbelief in sight and silence crashes unfamiliar waves in the only fixed presence in your life. In the family's life.

Like Peter, your mother's "unbrooklike" babbling stretches the rift into chasm-like proportions for the angry and sullen group. Keeping afloat is paramount in this moment. The one who named you needs you to be. Tensions ripple with increased intensity as the ascending heat grips each in their own emotions. Beware. Neutrality, for love's sake, is key.

The whir of the oxygen machine pushing air into emptiness compresses those gathered around the rented hospital bed. The impermanence of the medical provisions on the dining room table-turned-caregivers station is a mocking chimera of the continuum of time and space. You knew this moment was coming, yet walking the River Jordan with arms outstretched hasn't been an experience you can recall in this life. Eyes rouged with dry pain while inelastic faces thrusting rye remarks as deadpan is the defensive strategy. Works. Every. Time.

The breadth of your physicality is needed. The separateness between your mother and her angry siblings occurs because you sweetly release the grip between their joined hands as the family gathers around their beloved looking for signs. A slight rise and fall of breast tissue. A grasping inhale. Darkened digits sprinkled with liver spots giving a twitch. The same hands that gave those twisting pinches in church when you wouldn't sit still in the pretty dress your mother bought for you are still. Mouth slightly ajar. Eyelids placed shut. *Who will keep us all together now?*

With an amplified click, you stop the whirring. You halt the hum of the air mattress designed to provide comfort in the last days of Eileen. As silly as it seems, you refuse to lower the bars on the side of the bed because abuse of a corpse is a thing, and she endured enough in her lifetime, you think. The death of the matriarch magnifies the infinite thought fractals. Her scratchy voice declaring, "I love you forever and one day." Her cries of "Mama! Mama!" You muffle the last conversation and images long enough to make the three essential phone calls: the on-call nurse with the hospice to mark the beginning, the trusted family undertaker, and Trevor.

Reverend Williams.

Reverend Trevor Williams.

Reverend Trevor John Williams.

Eileen and Liz's pastor. Your friend. Your alternative life fantasy. The yang that understands your yang. Obvious friend and blind spot foe that must come to do last rites and offer up obligatory prayers.

Leaving the house to make a call on your cell phone that could've been made indoors on the landline, like the other two, is the perfect excuse to escape from the heaviness. The weight of the unknown sags your shoulders. Your fingers quake while lighting your cigarette. A migraine and bleary eyes are to blame for picking the wrong number three times under Trevor's name in your iPhone. Should you call his home or his cell? Would the cell even be on at this hour?

A luminous new moon provides unwanted light as you finally settle on calling his home in hopes you won't disturb his wife and daughter. It is 1:33 a.m. His daughter has school in the morning. As much as Grandmom preached the importance of education, especially for black youth, you're sure she would hate to be an interruption in that process. The school year is in full swing in these remaining days of winter. March has come in like a lion, and left lambs slaughtered. The shepherd is no more.

You awake with a start. *When did I fall asleep?* You pray that no one notices the drop of slobber hanging on the bottom curve of your lip screaming to the world to pay attention to this moment of embarrassment via lack of sleep. You wipe your face, trying to unsee what has been seen. Smearing on a veillike persona with your hands, you smile when you see no one notices your plight. You gawk at the entrance to the DC train station like a tourist. Smile explanation: complete.

The weary travelers enter and exit the train zombified by time and money. Barely hearing any politeness, you marvel at how well you can spot rudeness in others. People bumping into one another and looking at the offending party as if they were owed an apology. Near-death stares for overhead rack space. At least your focus has shifted. There cannot be anymore dream reminders on this long ride. You've still got more than twenty-three hours to go before the City of Win(d).

Maybe you can get lost in the city a couple of nights. Find a club or a bar where nobody will shout your name in greeting. Not that you're a huge bar or club person, but freedom and desire call. There's gotta be someplace where you can stay loose making sure there are no lingering attachments.

You don't do well with attachments. You never have. It's a blessing and a curse. Because you don't allow people to get too close to you, you never bother to get too close to them. Trust is seldom shown by others. If they don't demonstrate their trustworthiness, why should you? People present themselves as friends or lovers, but then they exit stage left. You're left to continue, depending only on yourself.

Needing a distraction from your thoughts, you fall back on your own created playlist of music. The only solace in an illusionary world. It's time for something new to think about, especially because if you review your presentation one more time, you may make yourself sick with anxiety. Anxiety attacks are no fun, and you don't believe in them, despite the appearances they make on occasion in your life. They're as inconvenient as the insomnia that plagues you.

The only person who was any sort of help when Grandmom died was Rebekah. That "devil woman," according to your mother, who you grasped onto and screamed from the depths of your soul at Grandmom's transition. The aftermath wasn't pretty, but Rebekah was the one that stood to your back when a piece of home was ripped from your chest, bloody and bare. Who would you be able to trust now? To whom would you turn when you needed some old-fashioned advice? Like you do now.

Despite what she claims, Mom hated Rebekah. With your authority issues, you deemed her lovable. Rebekah could do no wrong. She was the salve to cover wounds you didn't know you had, like that old school New-Skin stuff that promised to restore any scars back to the original skin color, replenishing the dermis and epidermis that had come off your left leg when you fell off your bike while trying to pop a wheelie in the driveway behind your house with all the kids from your block watching. You let out a soul cry while being helped into the house by your best friend, Ruby. Grandmom cleaned it up and put on New-Skin. She made sure that you wouldn't have an open wound on your leg for the rest of your life.

Your leg still carries that memory like a photograph, forever ingrained in emotion, but never returning to its original form. You wonder how Ruby's doing. She's probably enjoying flying from this place to that with her job as an accountant fixing issues in her assigned region for a Fortune 500 company. Meanwhile, your own fear of flying led you to take a train. In the dying days of winter. To Chicago. Chi-cah-go! You could've been there in just over an hour by plane, but, like your grandmother, you refuse to fly, especially in the wintertime. Watching airline personnel deice the wings on a

747 before takeoff doesn't inspire confidence for a flight that would fly in the cold and possibly accumulate even more ice.

It's March 9, and you almost forgot the significance of the day in hip-hop. Your playlist helps though. The tough fading in and out of the sampled song before the beat drops on Notorious B.I.G.'s "Warning" reminds you that it's the anniversary of the celebration of his life as a man and a storyteller. As one of the greatest MCs of all time, in your opinion, you revel in his ability to carry on the oral tradition set to the twentieth century time-space continuum. In another year or three, it'll be twenty years since his passing. It will also be that long since you graduated from high school. *Yikes! Where the hell did the time go?*

You should probably see how Ruby's doing, but you don't want to be a burden. With her divorce and her father's death happening as an all-in-one event, she probably doesn't feel like being the Pooh to your Eeyore. It's a much easier task to find and tack on your missing tail on your own, you think. Rebekah would come in handy right now, but you don't want to go back down that road. You ended that relationship, but it wasn't easy. It was the first you'd had in a long time with anyone, regardless of gender.

Still, those long nights in the apartment you shared were made easier with her warmth. She watched and worried as you withdrew even further into yourself, trying to make sense of the tightrope act of grieving and becoming a replacement mother to Eileen's three children. They felt like orphans. At the time, it seemed no one understood that you felt like one too. Aunt Carole is the biological youngest, but being raised in the same house as your grandparents, you felt like their youngest child who was spoiled like the firstborn grandchild but treated like their children.

In conversations that followed Grandmom's death, you know that Aunt Carole understands now, but Rebekah understood then. Being asked years prior to handle the business that was mainly Liz's responsibility, you accepted the role, in theory. In practice, your efforts to maintain normalcy for the first holiday to come up were of a Herculean effort.

"Why are killing yourself?"

"I'm not *killing* myself, Rebekah. I just want to make sure Mom and Uncle have a good Easter, that's all."

"Really? You don't even like church. You're not even a member anymore—yet here you are, getting all geeked up for a service that you could care less about and packing clothes to change into later, just so you can slave away in the kitchen for a dinner they will probably pick at. I mean, babe, what the fuck is the point?"

"The *point* is that I made a promise that I intend to keep. I thought you understood that when I said that family comes first, especially now."

"That's not what I'm saying."

"Then, what the fuck are you saying, Rebekah?"

"Why are you yelling?"

"I'm not yell—I'm not *yelling*. I'm asking a question in a *loud* voice. There's a big difference, my love. Now, could you move from in front of the dresser please? I'm trying to get ready and be on time for service. Mom is probably sitting in choir rehearsal now and wondering if I'll even show up on this high holy day."

"Would you listen at yourself? Not one time have you stopped to think about how going back there after all these years of absence will affect you. I just don't want you to make yourself emotionally vulnerable trying to deal with the church members who will inevitably ask you about how you're doing and all. I love you, and I don't want you to—"

"Babe, if you love me, you'll shut the fuck up and let me do me. This is about what's best for me and my family. I don't interfere when it comes to your so-called family. Do I?"

"No, but you're missing the point."

"No, *you're* missing the point. I don't have time for your psychoanalytical bullshit right now. This is exactly why I hate dating women. Y'all wanna talk and share and cuddle and shit."

"You know what, Neicy? Fuck you! Do whatever the fuck you want! You do that shit anyway! Go on and try to act like you don't need time to grieve. Who the fuck told you that you had to be Superwoman and solve the world's problems?"

"First of all, I told you to *never* call me by that name! Second—"

"I can call you whatever the hell I want! Bitch, I'm trying to help your ass out!"

"*Bitch*? Grr! Really? You can go! I should've never told you what they called me as a kid, and I should've never been with ya ass in the first fucking place! I should've listened to my grandmother with ya old, broke, uneducated, no-goal-having, barely keeping up with those edges in a nearly nonexistent hairline, couldn't satisfy a wet paper bag, user-ass bitch! Get the fuck on witcha demanding pain in the ass self! I don't need this shit, and I certainly don't need you!"

"Oh yeah? You don't need me? Who else wants you, Savannah? Have you looked at yourself lately?"

"Da fuck are you tryna say?"

"I'm saying how the hell can I satisfy someone when I'm not even attracted to them?"

"You calling me *fat*? So you think you're some kind of prize? Before I gained this weight, I still had to teach you how to fuck because you certainly didn't learn anything before I graced your life with my presence!"

It is happening. *Again.* You can't stop yourself. Maybe somewhere you know Rebekah was right, but you don't want to let her know that. She always pushes your buttons before you go to church. Not that you very often, especially after the last church you attended with her, but when you do go, you'd like to have your mind right. How can you focus on the task at hand with all of her … *insistence*?

The two of you thrust insult after insult at one another as you continue getting ready. You're too stubborn to admit you're wrong and that you *do* need her. You need her more than your conscious mind can recognize. She's only trying to help you—so why do you do this every time?

You decide then that she's got to go. Your family doesn't like her. You don't like the person you've become or the person she tries to mold you into. You storm out of the apartment into your car and damn near screech your way to the corner. *I hope I have everything because I can't go back in there.*

You try not to think about her pending tears as you leave. You almost smacked the shit out of her, which would be domestic abuse. You refuse to do *that*—no matter how tempting. Today is the celebration of the resurrection of Jesus. Grandmom would want there to be a nice family dinner where the family comes together in thanksgiving and celebration. You will not allow an outsider to derail this.

Never.

Biggie's "Suicidal Thoughts" comes on. You pause the music. Deciding against replaying "Respect" featuring Diana King, you remove your headphones and dig around in your carry-on for a book to read. Thankful that you packed one of your favorite authors, Fiona Zedde, you consume yourself in the story that is "Hungry for It." The car you're in is quiet enough that you can get lost in another world for a while.

Maybe it's PMS?

You shake your head. It's not time for that yet. It is, of course, always time for a good read. You've read this book plenty of times before, but the possibility of romance, with fiery lovemaking, is an ideal that grips you every time. What is lovemaking after all? Two clunky, sweaty bodies flailing around calling out to a deity that may or may not exist? Then, the two of you cuddle and share your dreams, hopes, and fears?

You'd much rather read about fantastical vulnerability.

Chapter 4

Nirvana Below

Somewhere between the Allegheny Mountains and the white-water rivers of West Virginia, you've finished your book. In the shuffle of passengers, luggage, and conductors, you've managed to feel more relaxed as the trip goes on. The winters in the past few years haven't been as dramatic as those from the blizzard of '96 when the mid-Atlantic was covered in more than three feet of snow. That was the year Ruby's dad requested barbeque sauce and your mom needed bread, but neither parent was willing to pay corner store prices. The two of you high-kneed your way to the grocery store across the street from the post office at Broad and Stenton Avenue, or Godfrey Avenue, depending on what side of Broad Street you were standing on.

That was a fun and exhausting trip, even for a couple of healthy sixteen-year-olds. By the time the two of you got back, it had been almost an hour. Ruby's dad was mad his girls didn't bring him a pack of cigarettes. He had forgotten that the stores stopped selling to minors on behalf of their parents because so many of youth were using that as an excuse to buy their own pack. You and Ruby were no exception.

You wonder what she's doing these days.

It is dark outside except for the occasional light post or illuminated sign. You've read one of your books, but you are in no mood to read another. It is just best to let your eyes rest as your grandmother would say whenever you caught her dozing off on the couch. "I'm not asleep, girl. I'm just resting my eyes." You knew to say okay instead of commenting on the light snore escaping from her thin, parted lips. She'd only hit you once in your life, and there was no reason to repeat the massacre against your face.

Music is and always will be the salve for the spirit. That special inner sanctuary that remains untouched by the experiences known as life. That's why you pick music based on your mood. It's about what you wish to remember. What makes you happy. Perhaps that's too highbrow for the fact that most of your musical memories from your teenage years up to the present include sex.

Sex. Physical gratification for playing the game. The feeling of dancing the most intimate of dances. Sex is the reward for the two-step of the verbal tango known as flirting. In your case, however, flirting is the pregame. Like Marshawn Lynch, you don't believe in postgame conferences.

Aside from your first love, you only gave one to Rebekah. You can't remember your grandmother and her final days without acknowledging Rebekah and her contributions. Even if they are forever cast in the shadowy haze of her gaslighting techniques. Beyoncé's "Diva" plays.

You never cared for that song.

All flash, sass, and little substance, Rebekah was the glue that held you together in the early days post-Eileen. Her speech and actions much later gave rise to the same roughness of sandpaper against nicked maple—never quite removing the nick and adding more dust than the years-neglected piece of wood in question.

Settling with the playlist that you made for your dance sessions with the girls in the youth group at church, you play "Grown Woman." Beyoncé's self-titled album, with the accompanying videos for each song, was the first album where you could play all the songs straight through since Jill Scott's "Who Is Jill Scott? Words and Sounds Vol. 1." The only other artist who had accomplished that feat, in your world, was Mary J. Blige. Pick an album in that case. Well, before the whole Kendu thing. He seems as helpful as Rebekah. What makes women pick the one person to share their lives with the most unequal person for them on the planet? And stay there for years?

Just because you love Rebekah, you spare her feelings. Attempting to be painfully loyal to the idea of a steady, monogamous relationship doesn't stop you from wondering why passion has passed you by like the angel of death passing over a doorway marked with lamb's blood. Your exodus into monogamy leaves you wandering, lost and on autopilot, in a desert of your own making. Fear of the dreaded "I told you so" from your mother doesn't help matters. This is how you ended up in this time. This space. In his arms. Searching. Wanting.

Even if it is a damn lie.

Moisture is in the summer atmosphere. It seeps between your thick thighs as alcohol has intensified your quest to quench your thirst. You can smell the intensity of the pending thunderstorm for Philly and the surrounding tri-state area. You'd love to go to the shore and walk the boards, but tonight isn't the night for a random drive to Atlantic City or Wildwood. It's one of those nights where you and Trevor get together for one of your marathon talk sessions over dinner instead of the usual breakfast or lunch.

Discussions range from religion to spirituality to politics to blaxploitation movies to family to marriage and relationships to family. The ability to have deep, meaningful conversations is something you've missed in recent months. Maybe years. Intellectual stimulation is and always will be a plus in your book. You know he has three older sisters and no brothers. *Are any of them into women by chance? Could he give Rebekah lessons on how to be a stimulating partner? In every sense of the word? Is that a thing?*

The alcohol-laden drink, which Trevor insisted you try, begins to make your head swim. You haven't eaten since two o'clock. And the waiter in this cozy Chinese-Japanese fusion restaurant in Jenkintown hasn't bought out your entrée. Knowing better than to finish the drink, you sip slowly until you can flag down someone to bring you a glass of water.

Luckily, Trevor ordered some steamed dumplings as an appetizer to share while your conversation winds down the road of truth and discovery with lampposts of humor lighting the way. The light-headed conversation continues as your food finally arrives. You've never seen Trevor so relaxed before. Maybe it's the alcohol—or the sense of freedom from nagging women.

Looking in his eyes, there is a sense of something neglected. Rejected. The windows into both souls mirror something else. Something more. There is a tall, potted plant akin to the ones you helped Mom throw out after Grandmom passed because, well, no one else really had a green thumb like she did. You break your gaze into his deep brown eyes and focus on the plant. Deep down, you sense that your eyes match the healthy green hue of the plant.

Whether it is from the conversation or the alcohol, you aren't sure, but a familiar feeling settles into your bones. You stretch your limbs and let out an obscene, almost moaning noise in the process. Trevor's eyes perk up, but they never meet yours as he fumbles to pay the bill. You knew what it is. You always have—every time you do it.

The interesting thing about the pastors who have served at the church is that they are men first. You found this out at fifteen when the pastor and the minister of music shared a steamy kiss when they thought you'd left for home. You were waiting for Pop Pop to come pick you up from Handbell Choir rehearsal as the last one to leave. You always walked as quietly as your grandfather. It was a skill you'd worked on, especially with ballet lessons since the age of four.

You knew which spots to avoid in the worn carpeted floor so you wouldn't be detected. Both headed to the office and back to the choir room. When the minister of music came back in and found you there, she was shocked and blushed. You never said a word about what you'd seen. Two months later, they'd both announced they were moving on to other congregations. The pastor's wife never knew a thing, and the minister of music went on to become a pastor herself. Guilt can be a motivator toward salvation. The jury is still out on whether that's a good reason to do anything.

Trevor, with his wife and daughter, was no different. How many times had the two of you discussed how certain female members could use some covering up with their low-cut blouses and sausage-skin dresses and skirts? These conversations were the reason you made sure to dress appropriately for fear of a church member seeing the two of you and starting rumors where no foundation existed for such things. The two of you were good friends, and you loved his daughters like they were your own. Well, that youngest one was a handful, but that wasn't your business.

It was bad enough that Mom and Grandmom had decided that Trevor was much more interested in you than in his "old-ass wife." She was about twelve years his senior, and her age was starting to catch up with her. And that midsection. Not to mention that turkey neck starting. Yikes! Made you glad that your Irish roots weren't as dominant as the West Indian ones. You hated covering your neck like your great-grandmother in those old pics you'd found in Grandmom's room. You can see why it was necessary.

Perhaps it was the two of them, with their own sordid histories, that invaded your psyche. The power of suggestion isn't just some cliched colloquialism. You'd toyed with the idea for a while in your mind. Even made Rebekah strap up a few nights because penetration is a beautiful thing. There is no harm in fantasy.

Is there?

With a mumbled, "I'll be right back," Trevor heads for the men's room as the server clears the table. You check your phone. You need to lay the groundwork. Do the damn thing right. Don't care if this might be one of your little "moments," which have been on the rise lately, but you told no one. You'd worn out your Sugar Spoon, and you couldn't justify buying yet another sex toy to Rebekah. The alleged love of your life. The same love who'd come in more than once just as the sun began to kiss the sky reeking of vodka and pussy.

Hey, babe. What u doin'?

Nuthin' much. What u up to?

Just having dinner with Trevor.
Havin' fun laughin' and jokin'.
You know how we do.

Lol yeah I know.
How's he doin'?

He's good.
Talkin' about the same stuff as usual.
The crazy people at the church, music, movies.

Oh, yeah that's right. He loves blaxploitation movies
as much as you do.

Yeah, he does. We were tryna figure out when we
could get together to have a little mini marathon,
but we both have crazy schedules.

Yeah, true. I was chillin' with some coworkers. Why
don't you guys try to watch one tonight. I don't
mind.

Well, we could. But I know he's got his own life, and
I don't wanna impose because it's so last minute.

Well, it's up to you, sweetie. I trust you.
I know it's up to me, babe. Why would you say that?
Of course you do.

Because I'm so fantastic.

Oh, lord! Here u go!

You know you love me.

Sure, sweetie. Ttyl.

K.

As Trevor returns to the table, you smirk to yourself and slide your phone back into your purse. Of course, Rebekah would choose to hang out with her imaginary coworkers. It was probably the bitch she posted about on Facebook and then denied it. Ruby pointed it out because she thought you should know. And it was no secret there were no warm, fuzzy feelings between the two. Rebekah, as usual, used that to her advantage when defending herself with such vehemence that you knew it was true.

There were no multiple coworkers.

There was only one.

She'd even gotten a tattoo with this broad.

Her first one, which was supposed to be done with you.

Karma's a bitch, and shade is her sister.

"Are you ready to go, Savannah?"

"But, of course."

You walk out ahead of him, enticing him with each step. You are on the prowl, a feeling that hasn't come over you in a long time. Besides, you went through her phone. Some ugly, insignificant dyke with the ugliest blonde dreads you'd ever seen with a picture of your girlfriend's panties in her mouth, and the worst attempt at a smoldering look you'd seen since those romance novel covers with Fabio on the front.

"Don't hurt yourself, Savannah."

"Why? Whatever do you mean?"

"I'm married. Not dead."

"Neither am I, Trevor."

You never did make it to that movie. Trevor told his wife that the two of you were catching a late movie. Something about a Pam Grier marathon at a theater in Abington. You were surprised at how well he could control his voice considering your lips weren't exactly wrapped around the car's parking brake. And there was the matter of being in Fairmount Park as opposed to being nowhere near Montgomery County.

He presses end, throws the phone, and grabs a fistful of your locks.

Your cheeks hollow as you began, with fervor, to suck out his soul. One of the advantages of knowing so many gay men is learning how to please a man. And men are so easy. All anyone has to do is suggest sex. This doesn't always mean verbally. That's usually the last thing you do because with a bedroom glance and body language accentuating your natural curves, there's not much else that needs to be said by you than yes. If you so choose. After all, didn't Foxy Brown, the self-proclaimed "rap Pam Grier," say, "Pussy is power"?

You were tired of wasting yours.

Rebekah had no idea how to handle yours. You'd given in and had sex on the second date because you'd never intended to see her again. She was a one-night stand that turned into a five-year nightmare, which started around the year one mark and spiraled from there. She was a great way to satisfy your own selfish needs, and because you felt guilty, you stayed. Even through all the fumbled attempts at her trying to learn your body and your mind. Had she learned to understand your mind first, you wouldn't have ended up in this position.

Well, Trevor was a great pupil ay figuring out your favorite position.

Positions.

Multiple times.

You'd heard of folks throwing around the term *sapiosexual*. The one that means someone who is turned on by intellect or something like that. You weren't too sure because you were too busy arching your back until your head touched your heels inside of his spacious family van. That third-row seating being able to be put away and a handy blanket made even tantric sex possible.

Those minivans are so spacious, and for some reason, there is a part of the park that Trevor knows about, and you don't, where the cops don't patrol as heavily. This is no time to ponder why. You are too busy earning the gold in the Sexual Olympics. And you don't care.

With every thrust back toward Trevor, every moan, every grunt, you take back what has been lost. You have no idea what time it was—and you don't care. You are alive. You are powerful. You are in control.

When he decides to lie down and let you work, you knew you are in trouble. You ride him like you have been let loose from a cage. God can probably decipher you two aren't praying, despite Trevor laying prostrate at the throne. He's been pushing the walls of heaven and is determined to enter the heavenly kingdom. He is concentrating on finding God tonight.

He left the old-school R&B station playing in the background. The quiet storm mix is on, which is one of your favorite times of night. The DJ's sexy, low baritone voice goes from Marvin Gaye to Jodeci to AZ Yet. AZ Yet's "Last Night" plays, you broke your rule. Repeatedly.

Following your usual "fuck rules" is a way to avoid emotional entanglements. No promises of forever. No tomorrows. Only that moment. And by no means, is kissing allowed.

You want to know what you taste like on those juicy lips.

There is a deeper connection that is implied through kissing. It implies love's promise, which you knew is a farce. You live it every day, and so does Trevor.

You throw your head back like you have so many other times. You are open, receiving, taking. You rake your nails down his chest while and see that bright, white light just as Jodeci sings "Feenin'."

Trevor pulls you down to him. Those eyes. That mouth. His large hands and long fingers leave tremors in their wake along your spine. Seeking. Grasping. Wanting.

Needing.

You thank him for the night, avoiding his kiss. The damage has been done. You are prepared for Rebekah's wrath. It is 3:33 a.m. when you enter the apartment. After a shower and getting ready for bed, you sigh and shut off the light. It is four o'clock. The only things open at this time of morning are the hospital and legs. And Wawa. Always Wawa.

Cold sheets and no phone activity greet sleep with exhaustion and angry tears.

Beyoncé's "Rocket" plays as you try to figure out where you are. It's not Chicago, but you know you're a lot closer than earlier. In a few more hours, you'll be at Union Station, ready to find your hotel and get settled in your room. A new city, even for a few days, should change your perception of things.

Nirvana would be nice for a change.

Chapter 5

Aria in C# (Db)

After a brief cab ride, you manage to settle into your new digs for the next few days. The heat envelops you in your deluxe room at one of the top hotels in the city as you sink into the king-sized bed, flip on the television, and check out the channel offerings. You've decided that ESPN serves as the best background noise for the moment. Free agency for the NFL is in full swing, and you enjoy seeing the highlights from the past season as the analysts discuss players, teams, and vacant coaching/GM positions at a lowered volume. You need to make three phone calls. Well, two. Ruby's at work, so you text her first to let her know you've made it safely. Your next foray into communication requires some deep breathing.

"Hey, Mom. Just calling to let you know I got here okay."

"Hey, Niecy, baby! I'm glad you called. I was getting worried."

"Mom, there's no need to worry. It's not as if I was going from Broad and Olney to City Hall on the Express. It takes a little longer than that to get to Chicago."

"Girl, I know that. Can't a mother worry about her child? Her only child? The one she had to travel in a blizzard to get to the hospital to have? The pride and joy of her existence? The—"

"Mom! I get it. And please don't call me that."

"Well, you had a praying grandmother, and now you have a praying mother. I'm glad Jesus surrounded you with his angels of mercy and granted you traveling mercies. I was praying about that. People are crazy, baby."

"I know, Mom. I grew up in Philly, so I'm not afraid of traveling to other cities. People are crazy everywhere. Hell, I made out just fine in New York City, so I think I can handle Chicago for a few days. Besides, it's not like I'm going to the South Side or anything. I'll be downtown where I'm sure there's the usual things: homeless people, crazy folks, people in a rush all the time. You know, the usual."

"Yes, I know, baby. I can call you that, right?"

"Yeah, Mom."

"I know that's right! Don't forget, girlie, that I'm still your mother."

"Girlie? Ha ha! Are you Grandmom now?"

"Ha ha! Hey, I can't help it if I sound like her. Just call me Eileen Jr."

"Ha! No thanks. I'll stick with Mom or Elizabeth, thank you very much. Besides, that's too many E's. Elizabeth. Eileen. It's too much to process for my mouth."

"Well, I like it."

"Yeah, great. So I'm gonna call Aunt Carole and see what's up with her."

"Oh. Yeah. Her."

"Here we go. Why did you say it like that? She is your sister, you know."

"I think I know that better than anyone. Does she?"

Deep breath in. Jesus, be a fence. "Mom, it's been almost three years. You need to move on."

"I've tried, but she just does whatever she wants. She's so selfish."

"Mom, I'm not going to get into this with you today. Just because you're the oldest female in the family doesn't mean people have to automatically listen to you. She's an independent woman who lives her own life as she sees fit. Why does that bother you?"

"I didn't say she had to listen to me, but I am her big sister. I'm just trying to be the best big sister I can be to her, and she won't let me. And I've got no problem with her being independent. I would think we, as independent women raised in the same house, could get along as adults, especially with our parents gone."

Independent? What kind of dream trip is she on? "Well, just give it time. I'm gonna call Auntie and see if she can tell me some good places to go around here to get some good food and see some sights while I'm in town. I'll talk to you later, Mom, okay?"

"Okay, baby. Love you!"

"Love you too, Mom."

"I love you, more!"

Despite the chilly weather, which is to be expected, the day is passable for nice. Good, even. Maybe. You're not sure yet. It's one of those days where you're waiting for the other shoe to fall—or maybe an anvil from Acme Corporation with comedic timing for audience chuckles while what's wanted speeds away with a mocking "meep-meep." Right now, you desire an exploratory walk and some kind of nourishment before your stomach starts eating away at what little lining might be left in there. In truth, you remember that certain years were a blur, so who knows what's going on inside of you?

You heard something about some great things to do on the lakefront, and you set about a brisk walk even closer to the icy waves in hopes of finding food. The fresh air should help to stem the tumultuous trains of thought. You're here on business. It's not the time for an episode of "Who Struck John and Why?"

Thankful for not seeing your breath form within the atmosphere, you venture the thirty-minute walk to Navy Pier. Grandmom always used to call you an airhead because of your sign, but as the "water bearer," you'd much prefer a body of water over air travel. That's why you don't fly whenever you can avoid the hassle. Between the TSA garbage and a couple of flights that had you calling for any deity that would listen, you haven't taken a flight since 2011 when you went to visit your future in-laws in Wisconsin at Rebekah's insistence.

Because walks go a little faster with music, you pop in your headphones, open your streaming service, and find one of your favorite artists and albums. One of the nineties trio of superstar female solo artists, Brandy, is always at the top of your list. If Aaliyah were still around, you're sure you'd listen to whatever she created. As it stands, Brandy, Monica, and Aaliyah will always have you as a fan. Of their music, anyway. Skipping the first six tracks, you choose "Focus" from the Afrodisiac album.

Sipping the air in solipsistic silence, you travel along the streets crossing Lake Shore Drive finally arriving at the pier. The slapping of the flags against the shore gusts matches the intensity of the clanging from the beaded rings that secure the flag to the pole. The cling-clang slap-slap-slap anti-rhythm alters your movements as you assess the view. Stunning sights over the source of water, Lake Michigan, inspire a lung-filling breath you clutch until the loud exhale catches your ears over Brandy's "Sadiddy." Hoping no one heard, you move with swift steps toward a nearby park.

Like most urban cities, Chicago tries to clean up the ugly side of things from tourists. Doesn't always work though. While no city could, or should, produce the same amount of filth as Philly, Chicago is no slouch. You've stumbled into gloomy pastures where developers have secluded broken beer bottles and used prophylactics behind linked mini-metal triangles in a sick game of systemic simplexes. A lone icicle cleaves to the tattered "No Trespassing" sign as a low-flying pigeon narrowly misses your head, causing you to duck. Being tall has its disadvantages.

"'Scuse me, Miss? Miss?"

"Oh, I'm sorry. May I help you?" *Holy crap on a cracker. I need to start paying attention. Where the hell did she come from?*

"Sorry, hun. Didn't mean to scare ya."

"It's okay." *I think.*

"I saw you walkin' 'round here, and I had to come over."

"Okay?" *Why me, Lord? Does my face say please come talk to me? WTF?*

"Do you know Christ as your Lord and Savior?"

"Uh, yeah sure. Excuse me, but I have to get to—"

"Well, child, I can see that. It's in your eyes. God's gonna use you for something special. Your voice, I mean."

"I do sing, so thanks, I guess. Have—"

"Yes, my child. God is gonna use your voice to help heal the world. Be blessed, my young sista!"

"Um, yeah ... you too."

What the fuck was that? You wave politely and goose-step your way in the direction of a table in a restaurant with something to scrape the taste of confusion and annoyance off your tongue. You're not even home, and Jehovah's Witnesses are still finding new ways to bother you. You think that's what just happened anyway. You're not really sure. Every time it's happened, you've been at some church function, and it's usually after you've sang a solo or led some group or choir you were in for a selection or three.

The weirdest encounter, well, second weirdest now, happened when you were headed home from school one afternoon. You remember it well because you were in your early twenties and had just stepped off the 22 at Broad Street and Sixty-Sixth Avenue after a morning filled with business courses, including an Excel class and your Marketing capstone at Temple University. You were wearing your headphones when an older black lady with some serious Coke bottles with bifocals approached you as you exited the rear door of the bus. She recited some of the same nonsense you keep hearing these ten-plus years later.

You were thankful to escape that exchange without the usual annoyance at being stopped for some crap you had no time to entertain. This current one, much like the previous one, still leaves you unnerved and annoyed. All there is in this world is the journey we live. You're already using your voice by singing, on occasion. *What the hell else does God want? Shouldn't he be worried about other things in the world like poverty and racism and not me?*

You decide that you refuse to allow any more distractions from your main objective: food! This hippie-dippie nonsense is a nonfactor in your world. It's not that you're a nonbeliever in a higher power. You just aren't a fanatic about it. What's the point? Everyone only understands from their level of perception anyway—so why get involved in the drama of explaining yourself to anyone? Your relationship with God is your business. As far you know, you're good. If this lady feels better telling you that God will soon use your voice, who are you to rain on her parade? Let folks do what they do—just as long as they don't try to stop your progress, which, is still food.

It's 1:33 p.m. central time, but your stomach is stuck on that East Coast clock. You might end up with that six-pack you had in college soon if you don't get some food. And warmth. Your nose is starting to hurt from the cutting winds. The expression *cut your nose off to spite your face* crosses your mind. Perhaps you should stop being too proud and bundle up for once.

You notice the selection of eateries, but nothing is speaking to you just yet. The click-clack of the flags and the rip-rip of the wind are a strange comfort to your ears. The white frothiness of the wind-driven waves of the lake catches your eyes. You walk toward a spot near the railing and feel the cold of the bars. Taking an inhale and an exhale, you switch the music to Jilly from Philly. "Do You Remember?" from Jill Scott soothes your nerve endings as you look left and see a place with some promise. Maybe a hearty French onion soup and a cup of hot tea are just what the doctor ordered. You never know what you want to eat these days since your appetite pendulum swings freely on the spectrum of nourishment possibilities. Those options aren't your usual choices, so you head to a place with comfort food.

In a hundred paces or so, you're almost at the door when you spot a dead baby bird popsicle. *Poor thing,* you think. *You didn't have a chance in this climate. Then again, there seems to only be hot as shit and cold as fuck for weather conditions lately.* Careful not to step on this frozen chick, the outward opening door almost catches your face.

"Oh, I'm sorry, Miss. Wait? Neicy?"

"Leah? What are you doing here, cuz?"

"I live here. What are you doing here? Why didn't you tell me you were coming?"

"I just got in town on business. Where's the love? Give me a hug, girl!"

"Of course, cuz! Let's get out of the door though."

As the two of you hurry to get out of the doorway and end the annoyed glances from nearby diners, you turn off Jill as she declares her non-clairvoyant abilities in "Love Rain" as you soak up your little cousin's appearance. Leah is wearing a one-size-too-small heavy overcoat with all the matching winter accessories. Her makeup around her eyes is a little too thick, which must mean she's wearing her contacts. These contacts are the gray ones she likes to wear when she's trying too hard to be cute. At five foot four with her straightened, long tresses with light blonde tips showing beneath her hat, you figure she must've come into the city to meet some new guy for a date or meet some friends. Either way, her suburban ass stuck out like a thorn in the rosebush of Chicago like it did when she used to visit every summer in Philly. Her prickish ways disguised as wannabe street smarts and being so grown are exhausting, but you just want to see how she's doing since the two of you haven't had a chance to really talk since you broke up with Rebekah.

"So how have you been, Niecy? It's been a long time."

"Yeah, it has. By the way, I'm here on business, so it's Savannah, thank you, but I'm good."

"Oh, excuse me, Miss Fancy. Ha-ha!"

"Ha! You know I'm not the extra-fancy type. And look who's talking? You know you weren't born with gray eyes, girl! Hahaha!"

"But I look good though!"

"They do look nice, Leah. I'm gonna grab something to eat because I'm starving. You wanna join me—or did you eat already?"

"I was supposed to meet a friend here, but they couldn't make it. I was just gonna grab some food on the drive back home, but this is better."

The patient, smiling hostess leads you and Leah to a small booth for two near the back of the establishment. Thanking her, you and Leah proceed to take off your winter gear before settling into the worn seats with springs that were once designed for comfort. It takes a beat or two to find a good spot in your seat before you open your menu while Leah clasps her hands together, providing heat with her tepid breath. You crack your knuckles, and Leah cringes. She never liked when you would do that. Being eight years her senior, you do it anyway.

The college-aged waiter brings water and waits as you order hot tea with lemon and honey and Leah orders a hot chocolate with whipped cream. Once he leaves, you smile at your favorite and only first cousin. The two of you were "thick as thieves" like Grandmom used to say. Leah used to follow you everywhere—even into the bathroom—when you were growing up. You didn't mind because as long as she didn't snitch on your happenings, she could tag along. Besides, who wants to stay in the house with nothing to do all the time with the adults?

Between your grandparents arguing more aggressively than not, Uncle Alex's teasing that could gallop over the lines of good-natured, equestrian-style ribbing, and your mother's, well, there was always that garbage. With your breakup and trying to piece yourself back together, you haven't been in communication with too many people. The cocoon of your own space was much more welcoming than the conversations that come after ending what was meant to be a long-term relationship with marriage on the table. Taking a long sip of water, you're eager to find out what Leah's been up to.

"So what's been going on? Last we talked, you had started a new job at a place you found through a temp agency that wasn't too far from your apartment. How are things?"

"Oh, wow. We haven't talked in a while. I did work there for a while, but some chick had it in for me, so I quit. I found a different job, but there are so many haters. So now I'm in business for myself—just like you."

"Wow. Sorry you had such a tough time, cuz. What's your business?"

"It's okay, girl. You know I'm not the one to deal with people talking to me like they're crazy, so I had to cancel some bitches. I had to walk away from the corporate bullshit."

"Please tell me you didn't actually curse someone out at your job."

"Hell yeah, I did! Every place I go, there's always some bullshit, and I refuse to deal with it. So now I've started a laundry business out of my apartment. I wash people's clothes at my complex, and they pay me."

What in the actual fuck? This girl? "Oh, okay. Does the complex know you're using all that water? And how does that work? What's your plan?"

"Good God, Savannah! You sound like my mother. 'What's the plan? What's the plan?' Is that all y'all ever think about?"

"Well, yes, when it comes to taking care of yourself financially and otherwise. I didn't ask you for a PowerPoint presentation or an Excel spreadsheet. I was just wondering what your plan is to grow your business. Maybe I can help get the word out or something." *Not even ten minutes, and this girl is on go!*

"Sorry. I'm just irked because all Mom does is drive me crazy with all her questions. I can take care of myself. I've done it all these years."

"I know you can. I just want to make sure you're successful and happy—like your mother does. That's all."

"Oh, I am happy, cuz. I'm dating someone new, and she's got it all together, girl."

"Really? I'm happy for you, but since when did you start dating women seriously? I thought those flings when we were both on the football team were just flings. You actually like women?"

"Weren't you the one who came out to me at fifteen? Aren't you bisexual? Why can't I be?"

"Whoa. I didn't say you couldn't be. You can be or do anything you want. You know that I'm not the one to stop you. I just didn't think you were really into it. I thought you were just figuring yourself out like we all are, cuz."

The waiter brings your hot beverages and takes your orders. You order the soup and a sandwich, which should fill you up until later when you're set to meet your new client for dinner and drinks around seven tonight. Leah orders a bacon cheeseburger and fries. At one point, that was your favorite meal. It was also how you gained so much weight during your relationship. You add the tea bag of herbal green tea while Leah tries to cool off her upper lip from her drink. She licks the whipped cream from under her nose.

"Well, I really like her. Plus, men are garbage. I had to switch teams."

"Hold up. Not all men are garbage. And that's not a reason to start dating women in a serious manner. Women who love women do so because that's who they are naturally—not because some man broke their heart, they're not attractive enough to get a man, or whatever other societal brainwashing nonsense is out there."

"Oh God! I don't need a mini-lecture, Savannah. I'm just saying that I decided to open my dating pool. You have to admit that women are more attentive to your needs than men though."

"Girl, whew, I'm not the one to cosign that either. I've been single for almost a year after a very damaging breakup because Rebekah wasn't attentive to my needs. She just played like it while she wanted to spend money and control my comings and goings. Dating the same sex doesn't mean you avoid relationship problems."

"I guess because the others didn't work out. How's Cherie, by the way? Y'all still friends—even after the way she treated me?"

"She's fine, I guess. I haven't talked to her in a few weeks because we're both pretty busy with work and such. Honestly, I had nothing to do with y'all's relationship. She's still my friend because she's been there for me when I've needed her and vice versa. And didn't you cheat on her? Repeatedly?"

"If she was taking care of her business, then that wouldn't have happened."

What the hell did I agree to? "Hey, that's your life and your business. So what else is new?"

"Not much. Mom moved to Georgia, so it's just me and my bae now. What's new with you? I feel like we've been talking about me the whole time."

Because we have. Narcissistic ass. I remember why I'm glad I'm an only child now. "Hmmm. Well, I've keeping a steady list of clients and gaining some new ones, which gives me the ability to focus the right way on making my money and working on some possible investments."

"Okay. That sounds good. What else?"

"And I've been volunteering at the church teaching the girls how to dance. That's been a pleasant surprise in my life."

"Why?"

"Because I'm not into the church thing, but I like giving back. Oh, you know Trevor is moving soon."

"Really? He's not gonna be pastor there anymore? Why?"

"He's tired of the drama. Being the first black pastor with a white wife over there can be emotionally taxing. I'm thinking of relocating myself, but I'm not sure where. Right now, I'm just gonna finish out my obligation to the youth group 'cause when he bounces, I'm gone. I don't have any ties to that place anymore. It was great growing up for the foundation it gave me, but I need to do something … new. Something different. Ya know what I mean?"

"Yeah, I guess. What do you want to do?"

"I don't know yet. I've lived in one city my entire life. I need a change."

"Well, what about dating someone? You seeing anybody special?"

"No, nosy. I'm not ready to date just yet. I need to focus on getting back to me first. The last three years haven't been easy with Grandmom passing and the drama that came, and then having to break-up with Bekah was a lot."

"Girl, you're getting old. You know you need somebody to come and knock them ankles loose, cuz! Ha ha!"

"Uh … not right now. I'm good."

"Oh, come on! I know you've got somebody who's been breaking you off. I know you."

"Nah, cuz. I'm good. I live a boring life."

"Sure. Sure. Have you even talked to Bekah since y'all broke up? She was so good for you."

"What planet are you on right now, sweetie? When I'm done, that's it. I don't keep giving chances, and I don't keep talking to a brick wall. I hope she's living a blessed life because I'm too busy living mine to care what the hell she does. I wish her well."

Finally getting your food, you and Leah stop talking for several minutes. You have to remind yourself to breathe and chew so as not to swallow the food whole.

Leah ends up choking on some fresh-out-of-the-fryer fries because she's also eating a little too fast. You sip your green tea before diving into the soup and taking a huge bite of your French dip sandwich. The au jus softens the bread as it slides over your taste buds, down your esophagus, and into your quieted stomach. Life is too short not to savor your food, especially after such a long day so far. Maybe that nap you missed earlier can happen before your dinner meeting.

"Are the fries that good that you can't take the time to chew, girl? How long were you waiting for your friend? Wait. Is this the girl you've been seeing?"

"Ha ha! Shut up! Yeah, she was supposed to meet me, but she got held up at some staff development thing. It's okay though. I'm sure I'll see her later. I got that sauce! You know how we do!"

"Ha! Okay! I see you, cuz!"

"Well, you know, I gotta represent for us Brown girls! We got that fire!"

"Oh, lawd! Your last name isn't even Brown, but I get it. Do ya thing, cuz!"

"Trust me. I am."

"How serious is this relationship? Should I meet them? We've both had our share of interesting relationships."

"Maybe you should meet her. I'll ask her what her schedule is, and we'll see if we can set something up. It probably won't be 'til the weekend 'cause she's an elementary school teacher. Special ed, to be exact."

"Oh wow! Okay! She's clearly dedicated because I couldn't see myself in that kind of a position. I don't think I'm built for that. Kudos to her! And in Chicago too? I've got some folks from school who are schoolteachers back home, and I know they go through it in the school district. I'm sure there's not much difference here."

"That's so true, but I don't care about that. All I know is that she's always been good to me, so it's whatever. She's someone who I can always count on—no matter what."

"Man, she must be something. How long have y'all been going out?"

"Well, we've known each other for about five or six years or something like that, and whenever I've needed her to stand to my back, she's always done so. And she does those things that Cherie wouldn't or couldn't."

"Okay, cuz. If you're happy, then it sounds like a good thing to me. Do I get a name? A picture in your phone? Something?"

"She goes by B. And I don't have any pics in my phone because this is a brand-new phone. I just got it a couple days ago actually."

"Girl, you're still going through phones. This one has a shiny, bejeweled case like all the others too."

"But, of course. A princess like me should have shiny things. It's only right."

"Ha! Girl, cut it out. You've liked all shiny things and surfaces, especially mirrors, since you were a baby."

"But that's because I'm so beautiful to look at."

"Leah, I'm trying to eat. You just spilled some ketchup on your shelf, by the way."

"Dammit! These damn boobs will be the death of me. Now, I've got a stain on my cute blouse. Oh well! I'll just make B get me a new one."

Really? "Uh, don't you wash other people's clothes for a living? Can't you just put some water on it and blot it until you get home or something?"

"What? Yeah, I should do that, but there's always a reason to go shopping. This one is perfect."

"Okay, but schoolteachers don't make a lot of money—unless you know something I don't."

"Girl, no, she doesn't, but whenever she goes shopping for work or her classroom, she always brings me something. Why should I stop that?"

"Hey, do what you do, cuz. I'm full. I guess I should box this up to go. How's your burger?"

"Delicious! But it's almost time for school to let out, and I don't wanna be stuck in traffic, so maybe I should wrap this up too. I'll eat these fries while they're still hot though."

"Yeah, it's never good to try to reheat fries. They suck when they get cold."

On cue, it seems, the waiter comes to check on the two of you and puts the check on the table. He's probably ready to close out his checks and go home, so you and Leah ask for boxes and work on splitting the bill. Leah only has dollar bills, and she left her debit card at home, so you pick up the check and tell her to leave the tip. She puts down a dollar and starts digging for change, which you hate. *Why do people try to undertip?* "Leah, what are you doing?"

"I need to pay the toll to get back home, so I don't wanna leave all of my money, Savannah. We can't all be ballin' and so perfect like you, big cousin."

"Why the sarcasm? I'll just take care of the tip. I may want to come back here another time, and I don't want the servers to spit in my food because you leave a shitty tip."

"Hey, I'm just trying to get my business off the ground."

"I get that, so just say that next time, silly." *Are we still doing this when I'm about to hit my midthirties—and she's at the quarter-century mark? Really?* "I've got you. Just let me know when you want me to meet your new girlfriend, okay?"

Leah starts bundling up as the waiter brings the boxes. She hurriedly packs her food and prepares for the elements, and you say your goodbyes. You watch as the stronger winds pick up her scarf, whips Leah in the middle of her face, and plays Grand Slam-level tennis with the hair underneath her knitted hat. You finish the water and head to the ladies' room to go before you make the trek back to the hotel. There's nothing worse than when the cold hits you and you need to pee when there's not a close enough or clean enough bathroom in your immediate radius. Collecting yourself after washing your hands, you head back to the table.

"Um, hi, Savannah."

"Rebekah?"

"Now, I know what you're thinking, but—"

No conversation necessary. You leave. Coat unbuttoned. Hat and gloves flapping in your left hand. Pushing the door open with your right. Tears of hot hurt and anger, unexpressed, slide down your cheeks only to damn near freeze in the whipping winds.

Leah?

Rebekah?

Leah and Rebekah?

Cousin and ex!

Chapter 6

Savannah, Do You Know?

D ear God,

I know it's been a long time since we've talked—or in this case, since I've written down anything. Let's cut to the chase. I haven't talked to you because I figured you stopped listening—or maybe I did. I took the first flight home because I couldn't take it anymore. After all the years of trying to do the right thing and be the right person for everyone, I get the pleasure of seeing my cousin, my baby cousin, and my ex together. There was no amount of money in the world that would've made me stay in that godforsaken place a minute longer.

What did I do to deserve such treatment? It doesn't even matter to me that I look like a piping-hot mess on this plane. I hate flying, but it was the fastest way to get home. I know the new client is gonna be pissed, but I couldn't. I can't.

As if I don't have enough on my plate, Grandmom's gone. Her children act as if they're the only ones who lost someone. She didn't give birth to me, but I feel lost. Abandoned. Alone.

Not one of them, even after the estate was settled, asked me how I was doing. How are you feeling, Savannah? That would've been nice. Instead, all I got was "she did this" or "he didn't do that" or whatever other crap they made up in their minds. Meanwhile, I had to deal with a failing relationship, and the three people I looked up to the most growing up became crying orphans.

I tried to be the peacemaker. I tried to do what Grandmom had been grooming me to do for years, but I could only do so much. To somehow be thrust into the role of matriarch when all I really wanted to do was run. I wanted to find the nearest bar and drink until it didn't happen.

I am not Eileen!

I know Leah's the youngest, technically, but damn! I just want to go back to a time when I'd come home from school to Grandmom watching her stories on channel 6 in the living room, usually *General Hospital*. She'd greet me and tell me to change out of my school clothes and get ready to do my homework. I'd get four cookies and a glass of milk before I had to start my homework in the kitchen while she made dinner. My homework had to be done, or at least cleared off the kitchen table, before Pop Pop got home from work at five o'clock. Within fifteen minutes or less, dinner would be on the table, and the two of them would ask about my day. No TV. Just grace and then dinner. I'd have to tell them both what I learned that day. Then, after dinner was done, I'd either finish my homework or help clean the kitchen. We'd wash dishes together, and I'd have to practice my spelling words or times tables.

Then, it'd be time to get ready for bed, and no, I couldn't stay up to wait for Mommy to get home from work. My only job was to go to school and get good grades. Be a good girl. Eat my vegetables. Go to church. Stay out of trouble. Now, my job is to keep quiet and internalize my own grief, my own pain, and my own suffering because God forbid I say something to piss off one of the kids.

"Family is everything," she'd say.

Did family mean everything when I had to play peacekeeper like I was in the UN? Did family matter when Leah decided it was perfectly acceptable to begin running through my friends and my ex, Rebekah, like a dancer on *Soul Train* with a new partner every week?

"Savannah, you're the best," they'd say. "You were there for us. We really appreciate it."

I know they do. Well, Mom, Uncle Alex, and Aunt Carole do. Leah, on the other hand … God, I don't know what to do anymore. In all of this grief and sorrow, I've just been lost. I take that back. In the midst of me trying to figure out and know who I am and what I am, I lost sight of what was important. I acted out. Well, for me, I acted out anyway. I ran. I avoided. I avoided me … and you! I clung to the most ridiculous rituals ever in an effort to escape what has become of my life. Where's the beauty? Where's the fun? Where's the passion? Where's the love?

All I feel now is hurt and anger. If I didn't leave that restaurant so many miles from home and act on impulse, I wouldn't have been able to write this on this plane. In fact, I don't remember how I got back to the hotel. All I saw were blurred shapes and bursts of brightness as I made my way to the airport and onto this plane. Am I so lost in my own thoughts that I'll accept being second fiddle in a married man's life? When did I decide to accept that it was okay to not have a personality—to just be a good girl and take it without complaints?

God … Savannah

Chapter 7

Satan's Soliloquy

Normally, I wouldn't bother to think or talk about my petty problems, but I'm starting to think that if I don't, I'll end up in a psych ward or in jail. I came home quietly. No fuss. No muss. Not even a phone call to my mother. There was no point. What am I supposed to say? Hey, Mom, I'm coming home early. I lost a chance to earn some money, and I saw your niece. She just so happened to be with my ex.

No, Mom, I didn't ask her if she got your card. Just didn't seem important at the time. I don't think you get that they're in a relationship.

No, I'm not mistaken.

Yes, I know you thought Rebekah was the devil reincarnated, but it takes two, Mom.

Bye, Mom.

Fuck family! I'm sick and tired of being told that I have to be the bigger person, I'm the oldest, or you know how Leah is. Really? I've been home for three days. I've changed the batteries in my Xbox controllers, and the Eagles and Sixers have won so many championships that the damn software stopped showing my character going to the White House in each game.

Ruby's been calling and texting me for the past two days, but I haven't responded with anything beyond "I'm fine, sis. Talk soon."

Every time I think about picking up the phone or texting her to attempt to explain, I just cry. I can't cover it up. As soon as she hears my shaky voice, she'll ask me what's wrong, the dam will burst open, and she'll be trying to figure out how to find large contractor bags, lime, cement, shovels, and a nondescript way to get to Chicago. As I'm typically the calm one in situations, I can't promise that I would stop her. That I would want to.

Mom called me once, but I let it ring. She left a voice mail, but I haven't listened to it. I don't know if Leah told her mother about our encounter, and she told my mother, or if Mom is just doing her usual checking in. Either way, I'm not in the moved for the blessed and highly favored speech right now. That's not to say that I'm angry at God, but I'm just wondering is karma a thing? Is this some karmic crap from a previous lifetime? Am I being punished for a past life? For this life?

Sure. There was the time when we were younger at an arcade, and I gave away all of the tickets Leah earned playing games. She'd gotten on my nerves, and I was tired of holding the bucket they were in. And there was the time I let her take the rap with Grandmom about who messed up her bathroom while showering, but was that really enough to do this? We were young. We were both only children and were almost like siblings when we were together. So some good-natured pranks and such were to be expected. I think. She wasn't an angel cither.

Leah would come for the summer, play outside with the younger kids, and somehow manage to run her mouth and start a fight. That kid would then go get their older sister or cousin or whoever, and she would come get me like I was trying to fight folks I grew up with. It was no secret that there were a lot of people around the way who I didn't get along with, but that's because I was never outside long enough to get to know them. My mom had me involved in everything from Girl Scouts to piano lessons and everything the church had to offer that was free or had a low/discounted cost to members. Ruby's dad was the same way.

We could hang out with each other—but not with the others because they wanted us to stay off the streets and away from trouble. Most of the time, we were helping out with Ruby's little brother and watching *The Box* or MTV until one of her parents got home—or we would take turns being on punishment. One week, I'd be on punishment for not doing my homework because I failed to see how learning about inverse functions, playing crab soccer, drawing, or writing a double-entry reading log was supposed to help me in real life. The next week, Ruby would be in the house for not doing her chores. I believe she hated cleaning the bathroom because she'd say, "What's the point? It's gonna get dirty again anyway." That always made me laugh because she knew she would get in trouble for it, but she just didn't give a damn. We'd purposely leave the block and go do something else because we knew once she was found out, she'd be in the house. Yet again.

A part of me is itching to go out into the real world—or I could be itching because I haven't showered or eaten anything homemade since I left. Nothing but takeout containers and empty soda bottles for as far as the eye can see. I don't even know what day it is. If I don't respond to Ruby soon, she'll come over—and I'm not for all of that. I think it's March 15. I know it's Monday, which is the day most people dread because they have to go to work. Any day that ends in y is a day I'd like to avoid.

People with their silly-ass routines of waking up early to go work for some person or faceless corporation that couldn't care less about you unless you don't produce whatever perceived need it's trying to sell to the masses. Never any time for lunch or real human interaction—until happy hour, that is. And even then, it's more about trying to drink away that last eight or so hours of a meaningless existence with two-dollar drinks and half-price appetizers in two hours that probably could've and would've been spent in traffic where you cuss and fuss about why people can't figure out how to merge into traffic from an on-ramp or how to use a damn turn signal—or when you're driving on 76 and trying to figure out who thought it was a great idea to let Quakers plan out the traffic patterns for future Pennsylvanians in the first goddamned place. Then, you finally arrive home and depending on where you live in the city of filth, you have to drive around to find a decent parking spot—or you're complaining because the one neighbor has two raggedy-ass cars that take up parking spaces but don't actually run. They manage to get those inspection stickers renewed every year though and clear the trash away from the tires periodically just so the city can't come and tow the vehicles.

I'm one of the "lucky" ones who live in an apartment complex with assigned parking spaces in a garage, but even that is a pain because visitors come and park in your spot. You have to figure out where the attendant is, and of course, they're on a bathroom break or an extended lunch break. The worst offender was the guy who was always on an extended break where he felt the need to take an abundance of tissues and hand lotions with him to the bathroom along with a fully charged phone with great viewing capabilities. Needless to say, he enjoyed pushing the walls of heaven in his mind in the bathroom and kept his job until it was time for an unannounced building inspection from the management because so many of us complained. Also, there was no way I was ever shaking his hand or wanted him to touch anything that belonged to me. If my car needed a jump, I just called a friend or my roadside assistance because … ew!

I should probably get up and do something with my life because I can't just allow myself to fixate on my ex and my cousin. That means letting someone live rent free in my head, and I can't have that. Doesn't mean it doesn't hurt though. I'll just do what I do best: distract myself with something else until I forget all about it. By the time it comes up again, it won't matter. I know at some point I'll have to see Leah because we are, after all, related. I have my doubts about that because I'm wondering where she learned about family from anyway. Maybe it's her daddy's genes. Shit! I'm doing it again. Time to get the hell up and get out of this damn apartment before the neighbors call about the smell, thinking I'm dead or something. Maybe a little on the inside.

Grandmom is probably rolling over in her grave if that's a thing. Look at the way her family behaves. Then again, Leah and I probably get it from our mothers. They tend to not get along, especially after Grandmom died. It all came to a head, which was just too crazy.

"Savannah, I can't do this anymore. Please go upstairs and finish typing this agreement. I'm done."

"What happened now, Auntie?"

"Your mother was probably running her mouth again. I keep telling Liz to stop all that talking."

"Your uncle is right, Niece. I refuse to sit near her while she keeps talking about what she's not gon' do."

"Oh, lord. What she say now?"

"'You can type up whatever paper you want, I'm not signing anything.' I don't care what you and your brother want. I'm gon' do what I wanna do.' That shit is pissin' me off, Savannah."

"Okay, Auntie, okay. You done started cursing, so I'll go upstairs, finish typing up the agreement, and print it off, okay?"

"I'm sorry, Niece, but I tried. If she says one more idiotic thing to me with her nasty-ass attitude, I'm gonna lose it—and I know Mom wouldn't want that."

"See, Savannah? I told you that I wasn't your problem. It was the two girls you had to worry about."

"Yeah, Uncle, I heard you the first fifty times."

"Okay. I hope so. I'll try to keep the peace, but Mom's buried now. You're gonna have to be the whole show around here, kid."

"Yeah, Savannah, because you already know that I need to go home. I haven't slept well in days. Lack of sleep and hearing Liz's grandstanding will make me lose my damn mind if I don't get the hell on that plane and go back to Palatine, okay?"

"I know. I got it."

Good God. Auntie is cursing, which is when you know she's angry. Uncle Alex is making sense for once, and Mom is in her room with the only computer in the house acting like she already owns the place.

You're standing at the top of the steps and wondering how you got up here so fast between trying to stop your quaking knees, beatboxing heart, and erratic breathing. You've always hated conflict, especially with anyone close to you. Here are three of some of the most important people in your life driving you to smoke a pack and a half of Newports a day because the oldest in years and not maturity is acting like a know-it-all, bossy, vindictive asshole. You just hope it's not genetic.

"Oh, so she sent you up here, huh?"

"I'm just trying to finish typing this up and printing it out so it can be signed and notarized, Mom."

"Oh yeah! I know. I don't care what you're typing. I'm not signing anything until I talk to a lawyer."

"Okay, Mom." During her rants, you know it's best to not feed into her bullshit.

"Puh! I know it's okay, Savannah. Mom wanted me to take care of the business, and that's what I'm going to do. *My* way! Do you hear me?"

"Mom, please stop yelling. I've already got us a lawyer, and she explained everything in detail to you. This agreement benefits everyone because there's no will."

"Why do you keep saying that? Do you think I'm dumb? I know that! I would just rather have another lawyer look it over."

"So you're going to pay for another lawyer to do the same thing? Honestly, without the agreement that Aunt Carole and Uncle Alex waive their right to the house, they could, if they wanted, claim their third of the property. I'd rather not delay getting these things signed and in place before Aunt Carole has to go back home."

"I don't give a damn about her going home. Shit! She can hop on her broom and fly away tonight if that's the case."

"Mom, please. Look, it's already done. I just finished printing it up—so the three of you can sign it in front of the notary who will be here this afternoon."

"So? I just told you. I'm not signing anything—period! I don't give a damn, Savannah!"

You've been shaking so bad from anger and frustration that you print up a copy full of misspellings and bad grammar. Instead of being able to flee from Attila the Ostrich, you have to remain a few minutes extra to correct the agreement. The faded orange and yellow wallpaper from the seventies reflects the misgivings of the longest occupant of this room. Struggling to stay attached to walls cracked from settling, the ancient wallpaper is either bubbled or falling or stuck so tight that you wonder whether camel toe is a possibility for a wall.

Your ears perk up at the sound of creaking stairs despite what are normally soft steps for Aunt Carole. You know it can't be anyone else because no one walks through the house like that since Pop Pop passed in 2001. Only his footsteps were barely audible within the house. This time, however, you know that Auntie has been not so silently brewing in the kitchen with Uncle Alex. The walls are thin inside of these row homes.

"Look, I've decided that you can just give me my paper back, Liz. I'll just go home, and we'll let the state figure it out."

"No. You already signed it, and I'm not giving it back. Besides, we all know that Mom wanted me to take care of the business anyway. The least you could do is sign that paper. It's not like you were here for anything else regarding your mother."

"Listen, I'm not here for your shit, Liz. Just give me the paper so I can go back to Illinois and mind my business."

"You mean take the money she left you, which I don't know why because you're already rich, and leave? That's all you do, Carole. You just come home, act like you're a part of this family, and leave when it's convenient for you."

"Really? Fine. Just give me the paper since you don't want to act like you have any damn sense. Sitting up here, laid across the bed with your legs kicked up like a teenager watching TV or playing Candy Crush as if you have no responsibilities and the world should wait for you to decide to do what's necessary because you don't like it. Nobody cares what you like, Liz. We have to follow what the state of Pennsylvania says because there's no will, so—"

"Why do you keep talking to me like I'm retarded? Do you think I don't understand?"

"You know what? You are retarded! You think you run things, and everyone has to do what Liz wants, which is bullshit! In fact, I think you've been a retarded bitch your whole life, Liz! Now, give me the paper, and I'll be out of your life and this godforsaken house forever!"

Somehow, you've slightly crumpled the agreement in your hand from your viselike grip. This ugly exchange has caught the attention of Leah, who was sitting in the living room playing on her phone and has come upstairs to see why her mother is yelling and cursing. No one cares when Liz is yelling and cursing. That's who she is. Always has been. Most likely, always will be.

Leah and you are bystanders in a situation that needed to be handled long before either of you were born. You catch each other's eyes in understanding. Neither of you feels good about family fighting, despite your own issues as cousins. You both feel Grandmom wouldn't want this but know it's necessary. Both of you watch in equal parts fear and delight. Mom has been pissing everyone off with her cocky, abrasive ways.

Aunt Carole has been looking at you with expectance to stop your mother. She knows that she shouldn't have gotten to this point, but after recent events and a lifetime of being hushed by their mother, she's had it. Her eyes plead with you to step in before something happens.

Liz, in her normal roly-poly fashion, manages to get up off her bed and stand with a menacing look in her eyes. You'd like to say that it's the grief clouding her judgment, but you know better as Liz's left fist connects with Aunt Carole's right cheek, grazing the bone, and narrowly missing her eye.

The fists and falling that happen are a whir in time. Leah tries to stop the fight by grabbing the folder with the paper, but Liz grasps her arms to stop her from leaving just as she's falling from the bed to the floor from Aunt Carole's blows and yelling. Liz ends up on top of Leah who struggles to get out from under those nearly three hundred pounds she claims can fit in a size eighteen. Between Auntie screaming, "You killed my mother!" and "Get off my daughter," you decide to call for Uncle Alex. There is no way you're getting in the middle of that, but you don't want Leah to be hurt under the pile of anger, grief, and frustration.

There's a certain tone that everyone in the family can recognize, so you use that at the top of your lungs. Skipping stairs like Carl Lewis, Uncle Alex comes in to pull the sisters apart just as Leah frees herself with the folder. Leah runs into the hallway and Grandmom's old room to take out the paper while Uncle Alex proceeds to pull apart his older sister and his younger sister. You allow him to take charge because, as a daughter and a niece, would anyone really listen to you? Would you seem as if you're taking sides?

As Uncle Alex leads Aunt Carole out of the room, you sit stock-still, barely believing what's taking place. Your emotions are laid bare in a moment that you know must happen, but you cannot ignore the devastation among your family. Devoid of anything except doing the right thing as Grandmom would want, you finally look at your mother.

Hair, a wild frenzy, with the look of a madwoman, she sits pouting on the bed with daggers dripping with anger and betrayal in her brown eyes. Her rouged face, small knot on her forehead, and stretched out black T-shirt are the only physical reminders of an altercation she began. With chest puffing in sorrow and disbelief, Liz does what she does best: lash out. It is, after all, the only thing that can give comfort in her time of need.

"Gee, thanks, Savannah, for having my back."

No problem, you think as you exit the room. *No problem at all.*

Aunt Carole was never one to bite her tongue, and Mom was never one to listen. I guess that's why Leah is more like Mom considering their birthdays are only one day apart. Maybe we're just destined to repeat this insane cycle. I have no idea, but I know that I'm making progress cleaning because I can see my rug. It could stand a good vacuum. Right now, I'm just gathering the trash before cleaning the place and then myself. Maybe I'll take a long bath, light some candles, put on some soft music, and just relax. Where's a jacuzzi when you need it?

With everything ready and a manageable warm water temperature, you decide to listen to one of your favorite albums: *Who Is Jill Scott? Words and Sounds Vol. 1.* Just before the opening track plays, the phone flashes a green light with a cacophonous ding. It's Trevor.

> Hope you made it okay. Lmk how your trip is going.
> I'm fine.
> Glad to hear it. Don't forget to think about what I asked you.
> I didn't forget. I just need some time to sit with it. We'll talk soon.
> Okay. Have a great trip! Love ya!
> Thanks.

I need to address the whole Trevor situation, but tomorrow is another day. Next week is another lifetime. This moment is about relaxing and getting my head together because I need to find a new client and some income sooner rather than later. To be honest, there is nothing special about sleeping with a married man. There is nothing good that can come from the cowriting of an affair and the pain it inflicts on all parties involved. Furthermore, there is nothing different about having endured a five-year relationship just because my pride would not allow me to admit I made a mistake—a mistake so loud that my family and friends were unsure of who I was when I allowed Rebekah's existence to overtake my own. All my family and friends, except Leah.

You sigh. *The only difference between me and Jill are the players involved. This is my life. The names and faces have been changed to awaken the innocent—or the stupid. How could I have been so stupid?*

Seeing Leah only served as notice that you do not wish to carve back the husk that has become your existence. To remove the veil of societal expectations and flawed binaries would be to look at the face of God herself. Life's experiences, full of scripture and twisted rhetoric, have left you shattered and bruised. Broken.

You notice a couple of smudges on the mirror's surface, but the worst part is seeing your own reflection as you peel off your horribly dirty clothes. *Who am I?* From the dawn of midnight to the half-crescent moon of tomorrow, you've logged gashes in your heart. The mere mention of Rebekah or Leah reminds you of this. Despite your best efforts to erase the time from your mind, the memories slip down your cheek. The bleeding of your soul has left you in hardened concrete. Pieces of light flicker in your watered-down coffee eyes. You should probably journal, but you'd rather just slip into the tub and be far, far away from here.

Where would I go? What would I do? Ruby told me in her infinite wisdom—that's what she likes to think when I finally ask her advice on occasion—that we all run toward lies. I'm not sure if that's true or not. I do know that I was never one to like conflict or anything uncomfortable—not even as a kid. Whenever anyone would argue in the house, I'd just shut down. I'd get quiet and sad. I need to get myself together. There's money to be made and things to do. After my bath, of course.

Chapter 8

The Queen of Avoidance Strikes Again

Precipitation palpitates against the window with a screaming wind as the voice of Darth Vader fills the room along with the lighted screen of the cell phone. *That's no one else but Ruby. If I answer it, I know she's gonna ask what's up, and I'm a bad liar. If I don't answer, she's gonna know something's up and keep harassing me until I answer—or worse, she'll call Mom.*

"What's up, chickie?"

"Hey, sis! What's good? We done playing phone tag now? Ha ha!"

"Ha! Yeah, you know I had to see how Chicago's going. And I need to hear this tea, bitch!"

"Ruby, I ... well ... uh ..."

"Damn, is it that bad, sis? What happened?"

"I've gotta sort some shit out, and seeing Rebekah and Leah when I was in Chicago did not help."

"What? What are you talking about? You mean you're back home already?"

"Yeah. I'm home."

"What the hell is going on?"

You explain the whole thing to Ruby and try not to add personal commentary along the way. Ruby, however, adds her own thoughts that you try to ignore. You just want to tell her what happened before processing anything. Venting helps as the tension in your right shoulder lessens. *Didn't even know I was that upset.* There's so much that Ruby understands, which comes from being friends for damn near thirty years. While what's understood doesn't need to be explained with Ruby, there's things that you've never shared with anyone, including her. It's not because of a lack of trust. You're just used to being the voice of reason. Normally.

"Oh, hell, no! Where's my shovel and contractor bags?"

"Chill, fam. It'll be fine. It's just crazy that she even had the nerve to say I was never there for her."

"Are you serious? That's some disloyal shit, Savannah."

"No shit! When Grandmom died, Leah decided it was cute to tell me that I do more for people who are not family than I do for my own family. Really, bitch? Then, when I try to talk to her about it like an adult, she wants to flip some shit around on me like I'm insane and play the damn victim. Again. As usual."

"Damn, sis. We know Leah has always been in her own world, but—damn—I know you felt some type of way running into her."

"Yup. Mom's been harping on family and how we should come together, but there's only so much of Leah's shit I'm gonna take—family or not."

"You already know that's why I don't talk to the unmentionable one. He's crazy."

"Oh yeah. Him. Your older brother is insane too, but that's another conversation."

"Yes, please, Savannah. What about your ex?"

"What about her? I don't wish her any ill will. Just leave me the hell alone. I take back the ill will comment. I hope she's on a slow fall to hell with cement shoes."

"Ha ha! Not cement shoes though!"

"Am I lying? Girl, please. Talkin' 'bout I miss you and shit. Girl, bye! You didn't miss me when you slept with that chick from work, did you? You didn't miss me when you flipped it on me, did you? And when you told me about her Facebook post, then her argument was that she was talking about me. Lyin'-ass bitch! I'm busy grieving for my grandmother while you're posting about how you can still smell her scent. Who the fuck was she talking about? Because it wasn't me. There was no sex in the champagne room for a while, especially while Grandmom was sick and then died. She was probably talkin' about Leah now that I think about it."

"That's as bad as my ex-husband. You know I get it, sis."

"What's worse is that in Leah's mind, she's not doing anything wrong."

"Are you kidding?"

"No, I'm not. I don't understand her logic."

"Girl, I got bail money."

"Ha ha! Stop. I'm not going to jail for anybody."

"You act like we'd get caught. Come on, sis! You know we haven't done anything in a long time."

"Yeah … because we're older now. We can't be running around acting all out of character and shit. I ain't got time for the games. I got money to make and shit to do."

"You mean you have things to see and people to do, right?"

"Ha! Cut it out!"

"What did I say?"

"I can't with you. You're a mess!"

"Yes, but you love me anyway, sis."

"Of course, I do, Ruby."

"Savannah?"

"Yeah?"

"You need a good distraction to take your mind off your crazy-ass cousin and her shenanigans."

"I've got enough going on. No thanks."

"You know what I mean."

"Ruby, I don't wanna be bothered with anything right now that doesn't make me money. If it don't make dollars, it don't make sense. I'm just tryna get things together for myself."

"I get that you gotta get your hustle on, but you need to release some tension like SWV. For real."

"Ruby, I've done enough of that."

"Recently? Am I missing something?"

"Ugh. You know Trevor, right?"

"Yeah? That's the pastor from the church, right?"

"Yeah. Him."

"Wait … did you do what I think you did?"

"Well …"

"My bitch!"

"That is not something to applaud, sis! It was a fuck. I didn't win the Nobel Prize."

"No, but after not having good sex for however long, I know you needed that release."

"True, but if anyone ever found out at the church, it would be a mess. He's moving away anyway. Thank God."

"Oh, that's right. He's married."

"Uh, yeah. It was once. Okay, twice. Just to be sure."

"Ha ha! What do you mean, Savannah?"

"The first time was after I found out about Rebekah and her bitch from work. The second, and I promise last time, was after Grandmom died. There was crying and alcohol and comforting and, well, you know the rest."

"Yes, but I want details! There's some juicy revenge sex that I wanna know about!"

"You're a mess! I've been on this phone long enough, girl. That's a story for another day."

"Boo!"

"I'm gonna go for a drive or something. I'm getting stir-crazy."

"In Savannah speak, that means I don't want to talk about it right now because I feel guilty as fuck. It's cool, sis. How long have you been home anyway?"

"Well, damn! Could you save the shade for later? And long enough."

"Reading comes before shade, bitch! And embrace the dark side of your personality. That's when you have the most fun!"

"Ha ha! Whatever, yo! That's why you've got the ringtone you do right now."

"What did I say?"

"Girl, bye. Don't you have work to do?"

"Savannah, it's four thirty in the afternoon. I'm headed out the door. Whatever work needs to be done should've gotten to me earlier."

"Damn, it's that late?"

"Do you even know what time it is?"

"Now I do. I'm gonna finish gettin' dressed. Maybe I'll go out and find some dinner while I'm on my drive."

"In rush hour traffic?"

"I gotta eat, sis."

"How about I go home and change, and then we go out to dinner? I'll call you when I'm on my way."

"Where are we going?"

"Our favorite place downtown."

"Then, I should look like a decent person, I guess."

"Chima has a dress code, so yeah, you should."

"Cool. Text me when you leave your house, Ruby."

"Will do."

Ruby always knows how to make me laugh. I do feel better now that I've talked to her. I guess I should answer Trevor and let Mom know I'm back in town. I know Trevor wants me to take over the youth group at the church, but I'm not about that life anymore. I was fine helping, but to become the whole show is just a bit much for me.

Who am I to be somebody's role model? What am I supposed to say to these teenagers? I know it looks to them like I've got it all together because I live on my own and have a nice car, but I really don't. I slept with somebody's husband. Twice. A pastor no less. He's leaving, and I'm not sad about it. I was never one for commitments anyway.

Chapter 9

Cracked Communion

Only Ruby could get me to get out of the house. For one thing, she's the only one who can see through my shit. She's also the only one who I let that close. And she calls me on my shit. Honestly, this will probably be the first and only time I'll be in the position of asking for advice. To keep it one hundred, I need something right now because what the hell is going on in my life?

I've never felt this way in my life—or maybe it's better to say that I've never acknowledged feeling this way. I'm totally lost. The only thing I do, whether it's out of habit or fear or both, when I'm feeling horrible is pray. And write. It's been a while since I've journaled anything. The truth is … I don't know what to say. I just keep it all inside because showing emotions, of any kind, is a weakness—at least it was when I was a kid.

I was the biggest crybaby around. I was always trying to just "make Mommy proud" like she'd say to me every day before I went to school, church, dance class, or pretty much anything that involved me leaving the house. I could be heading down the street to Ruby's house, and I'd have to "make Mommy proud." The sound of lofty expectations was deafening indeed.

It's a good thing I already took my bath, so Ruby wouldn't have to wait for me to pick an outfit. If I wear my all-black sweats, Ruby will think something's wrong. If I get too fancy, she'll know something's wrong. Why do I need to get extra fancy to hang out with my bestie? Then again, since I think we're headed to our favorite place downtown, I should look presentable. A Brazilian steakhouse isn't the place for Jordans and sweats.

I've got a walk-in closet full of clothes and shoes, a habit I picked up from Aunt Carole, but I don't have any desire to deal with this stuff right now. Even my accessories and underwear have to match. God, what a narcissist!

I'm guessing some nice pants and a clean blouse work. Since when did I get so many pairs of black pants? I've got to get some color in my wardrobe. Sheesh!

Ruby will be here sooner rather than later. She's like those commercials where the repair guy says that being fifteen minutes early is on time and on time is late or some such nonsense. Before I know it, she'll be pulled up out front of my building texting me "I'm outside," and I'll still be standing here in my fluffy magenta robe with the hearts on it, which has seen better days. It's my favorite though. Even with its frayed belt edges and fading white hearts, it comforts me—and it has always taken me forever to figure out what to wear.

My eyes finally settle on a cute short-sleeved blouse with some slacks and an open blazer. Now, I can pick out my underwear, shoes, and accessories. There's still the black, slim-fitting pants, but at least there's some color in my outfit. Ruby will clown me something furious if I go out looking like I work for the agency in *Men in Black*.

I'm feeling … I don't know how to describe it. Catching a glimpse of myself in the mirror (it hurts to look at myself these days), I realize I don't look too bad. At least my locks are in decent enough order to go out. They don't look like locks growing from out of an afro, so that's a plus. If I bothered with makeup, I might even be a knockout, but that's too much fuss—even for me.

After some careful arranging of my appearance and another brief look in the full-length mirror, I grab my purse, keys, and phone. As soon as I touch the phone, it dings with its little green light. I know it's Ruby. Her text says she's about five minutes away. In Ruby speak, that's really two minutes, so I spray some vanilla-scented perfume and head down to the lobby. Although my apartment is somewhat in order, I'd rather not have Ruby wait or have to come up needlessly.

Living on the fourth floor of this building isn't so bad, especially because the elevator doesn't take as long to show up. Sometimes, I like to take the stairs, but not tonight. I don't want to break a sweat. We are headed to Center City after all. With all the city's movers and shakers around, there's no sense in looking like I pushed Ruby's Jeep to the steakhouse.

The front of the building from inside the glass doors looks beautiful. The lights cast a brilliant shadow over the carefully manicured grass. Well, the grass that is trying to grow anyway. Pennsylvania's most famous groundhog predicted an end to winter sooner rather than later, and the birds chirping in the morning and the flowers budding forth are welcome signs as Ruby silently pulls up to the curb. My stomach flips and flops, and my breathing becomes shallow as I walk outside. It feels like those times when I know I've done something horrible, like cut school, and was hoping Mom didn't get the phone call before I did. Good God, what the hell is wrong with me?

Because it's always been a habit of mine inherited from my mother, I rarely look down when I walk. The effects are usually good, except this time. The front of my right penny loafer catches a rock on the sidewalk, and I damn near crash into the passenger door with my hands breaking my almost face-first fall. It's not exactly a smooth journey or entrance to say the least.

Seeing the faux look of concern on Ruby's face, I take a deep breath before opening the door.

"What's up, chickie? Have a nice trip? Ha!"

"Really though? You could've asked if I was okay first, bitch."

"Okay. I'm sorry. You okay, sis?"

"Nah. Too late now!"

"Tee-hee!"

"Go on and get it out your system."

"I've got plenty of time to do that. It's gonna take us a while to get downtown."

"Grr."

"Aw. You know I love you, sis."

"Yeah, yeah, yeah. I love you too."

Ruby pulls away from the curb expertly, considering it's still rush hour traffic, which should be dying down soon enough. Not enough yet though as we seem to be moving at a snail's pace. Then again, she always did drive like an old lady. Drives me absolutely bats. We're not seventy. "Put your foot in the tank and go," I wanna shout, but I know it's her Jeep—and she's just looking out for both of us. Besides, there's no point when as soon as we reach 76, I could probably cook us dinner while we sit in the remaining end of work day traffic. Worst expressway ever.

As Ruby babbles on about her day while weaving through street traffic heading to Lincoln Drive, I mumble cursory responses. Judging from her side eye, this is not lost on her. She keeps talking because she knows that I'm still processing my Chicago trip—and the fact that I chose to fly back, which I'm deathly afraid of in the winter. There's some other things that I feel I should share with her, but I decide to wait until we get seated to get into. It's much easier to speak when I'm stationary with food as opposed to watching the view and the crazy drivers on the road. Just then, some reckless driver with Jersey plates tries to cut into the next lane over, hits a pothole, and catches a flat.

"Womp womp!"

"Ruby, don't laugh. That could've been us."

"Puh! This ain't Jersey. Dumbass should know better."

"True. The potholes become craters. Like that Crittenden Street Crater. Fam, if they don't fix that soon, it might swallow somebody's car whole."

"You ain't neva lied, sis!"

We proceeded down the drive until we get to 76, which, surprisingly enough, was moving along at a steady pace. We might actually make our reservation on time. Ruby's a time bug, so that's no surprise. She finally asks about what's been going on with me, and I tell her that I haven't even told Mom I was home yet.

Clucking her tongue, she chastises me, but she understands. Whenever I travel, Ruby checks on Mom for me, making sure she gets to any appointments or gets to the store if she wants because she doesn't drive. Not that Mom can't drive. She has a license, but with her eyesight, she's always had rides everywhere. Despite my complaints, I don't mind—most of the time. It's her constant cheerfulness and damn near super-saved speech that drives me up a wall.

Because it's that in-between time of the day, Boathouse Row isn't quite as spectacular as it normally is when it's all lit up. At least we're almost to the restaurant. I can almost taste the food. I always get a kick out the gauchos as they walk around with the various cuts of meat prepared at varying temperatures for your choosing. Ruby likes the meat damn near rare while I prefer medium well. The blood from the cuts of meat tends to run into the mashed potatoes, polenta, and other side dishes on my plate, so I'd much rather have a little pink as opposed to the cow still mooing. Ew!

It takes another ten minutes, but we've finally arrived at Chima. It's our favorite place because parking isn't a problem. Whether you choose to do valet or park in a nearby lot, the service is excellent, the food is exquisite, and salad bar is quite fantastic. Since it's March and still a bit nippy outside, there are not as many people. To be honest, the only time I don't like coming here is during Restaurant Week. Although there's a break in price per person, it's too crowded, which affects service a bit. Obviously. I like to come when there's not an influx of folks trying to impress their dates by taking them to someplace other than Red Lobster or Olive Garden after getting their tax refunds.

Once we exit the vehicle and the valet takes the jeep, Ruby and I step inside through the revolving door and check in. We crack on people in the front and the bar area who have apparently never heard of a dress code before, but because happy hour is over in about five minutes, the crowd starts to thin out. As a precaution against Philly traffic, Ruby set the reservation for seven o'clock—just in case. My constant phone checking is starting to annoy Ruby from her distressed look, so I put it in my purse and focus on the street. JFK Boulevard is alive with the changing stoplights, pedestrians, people waiting for the 38 or 33 bus, and restaurant patrons entering and exiting Chima. I like to observe what's happening because it's easier to sit and make up stories about what I'm viewing than think about the traffic clogging my mind.

After a few more moments of mindless observation, we're taken to our table. It's on the other side of the frosted glass partition, so our view of the salad bar and the other patrons is obscured. It's a bit quieter on this side, and the few other tables, mostly for parties of two, are filled.

The kind waiter asks the usual question about if we've been here before, and we both answer yes. He skips the explanation of how things work and sends us off to the salad bar after collecting our drink orders. Ruby orders a vodka and cranberry, and I get a Long Island with top-shelf liquor. If I've gotta pay double digits for a single drink, I might as well enjoy it. I just hope we don't have the same debate when the bill comes. Although I'm a little older, Ruby always wants to treat me like I'm her baby sister. It's sweet, but I don't want it to seem like I expect it or am not appreciative of her having my back. Besides, as I always tell her, I may need her to pick up the check when I really don't have it. Tonight is not one of those times. Just because I didn't finish my business in Chicago doesn't mean I'm hurting by any means.

With a plate of cantaloupe, craisins, and fresh asparagus as thick as my thumb, I settle into my seat and wait with nerves on edge for

Ruby to get back to the table. An involuntary chill runs down my spine since this part of the dining area feels a bit chillier to me.

Ruby sits down after a moment with a plateful of veggies and whatever else she can fit on it. Her gaze fixes on me as she ingests some mixed greens.

I close my eyes and breathe deeply to calm my nerves.

"Okay. Spill it. What's on your mind? You've been unusually quiet—even for you, sis."

"I know. It's just … my life is a damn mess. I don't even know how to feel about it. Honestly, if you hadn't called me to drag me out of the house, I'd still be on the couch trying to win a third consecutive championship with the Sixers in my 2K game."

"You know you're in a dreamworld if the chip is back to back to back. The Sixers? They haven't experienced anything close to success since the 2001 Finals and AI."

"Ha. Yeah, I know. Even before the game gets to Hall of Fame level, it's not an easy thing. But you know that's how I think. I'd rather beat the hell out of a video game, sis."

"You mean than talk about and face what's going on. What is going on?"

"You mean aside from the whole Leah fiasco? A lot. I just wanna go home."

"Girl, we just left your home. What's really going on?"

"I—"

The waiter interrupts with our drink order. I've finished my meager beginnings and ask for a fresh plate while Ruby is still clearing hers. He trots off to get both of us a fresh plate, and I clam up until he returns.

Ruby waits with a patience I've only seen her exhibit with those she cares about. An Aries through and through, when she loves you, she's all in. When you cross her, she will deny your existence as if you're some random person on the street. It's one of the many traits we share. Ask our exes.

"I'm digging your outfit, sis. I like the purple. You've even got the shoes and purse to match your blouse."

"Thanks."

"It's about time you added some color to your wardrobe. The splash of off-white really makes it pop. Looking like royalty or something."

"Thanks. I don't feel much like royalty, but I appreciate the compliment, sis."

"I know. You don't have to tell me. I could tell on the phone, especially after you told me about your cousin. She's all kinds of outta pocket. What happened to girl code—or family even?"

"Don't get me started on that again."

"I'm not—not until we get going with the meal anyway."

The waiter and his assistant take away Ruby's cleared plate and give us fresh plates and side dishes. We ask for more of the rolls, which usually taste like melted, buttery heaven in my mouth. I attempt, in vain, to resist the urge to eat any. Ruby, never having been shy about eating, takes two and pushes the small plate with the remaining two in my direction. Her action demands I eat because she knows if I've eaten anything, it's been sparingly and probably a bunch of junk. We exchange a knowing look before flipping our little rounded cards from black to orange to indicate we're ready for the gauchos to come around with the meat. I rub my hands together not in excited anticipation but to chase away the coolness running through them from my fingertips.

"So continue, chickie. What's on your mind? There's no way you've just been playing your video game incessantly without something being on your mind. Out with it."

"Ugh. Fine. I'm a filthy, dirty, rotten whore who's selfish."

"So? What else is new?"

"Sis, I'm serious."

"What? I'm just saying. Remember when we used to go to the club and to parties all the time? You're not telling me anything new."

"Okay. Granted you've got a point, but that was harmless kid stuff."

"Wow. What did you do?"

"Not what. *Who.*"

"Okay. Who did you do?"

"Trevor."

I can't bear to look at her. Ruby's mouth agape, she drops her polenta onto the floor. I opt to stuff my mouth with a roll and bite into its soft baked goodness. It tastes like gravel in my mouth. I ingest a long gulp of my Long Island and take another bite. Doesn't help. Luckily, the meat starts arriving and is sliced and placed on our plates. One of the gauchos picks up what's left of the polenta on the floor after stepping on it initially before leaving.

With the short flurry of activity completed, we both turn our little cards over to black.

"Wow."

"Could you lower your voice please? We're not doing a podcast."

"Sorry. You just caught me off guard is all."

"I know. It's just, I mean, I didn't mean for it to happen. It just did, sis."

"Um … when did this happen?"

"The first time was—"

"Exsqueeze me? The first time? How many times—"

"Just twice."

"Oh, so you've become Mary Magdalene only twice. Forgive me."

"Don't start, Catholic girl."

"Sorry. I'm just shocked is all."

"Well, I get it, but damn. I'm already beating myself up at it is. I don't need any help on that front."

"You're right, sis. So when did it first happen?"

"A few months after Grandmom died. I went to dinner with him, and we were talking and having a good time as usual. Bekah was doing her thing, and Anna was being a pain as usual. I'm not offering excuses. I'm just painting a picture, okay?"

"I didn't say anything."

"You didn't have to. Your face is rather loud."

"As if that's not the pot calling the kettle—"

"Anyway ... we had a few drinks—pretty strong ones—and we ended up getting pretty deep into life and what it all means when you're married or have a partner. Of course, I started talking about how I was gonna leave Bekah anyway before Grandmom fell but didn't because I couldn't handle the stress of a breakup and caring for Grandmom at the same time. Next thing I know, we end up in his van stealing embraces of heaven."

"Don't make it sound all poetic and fancy, bitch. You fucked a married man. And he's no better cuz he's a damn pastor. Isn't one of the Ten Commandments "Thou shalt not commit adultery" or did all those years of religion class go to waste?"

"Yeah yeah yeah. I know, sis."

"So what happened after that?"

"He dropped me off, and I came home to an empty bed that night anyway."

"Hold on. What time did you get home? I mean, how long were y'all fuckin' anyway?"

"Keep your voice down and don't be so crude."

"If I wasn't so crude, we wouldn't be friends."

"Good point. I think maybe two in the morning. I don't remember. I didn't fall asleep until after four, and the bitch still wasn't home. She didn't get home until after I forced myself to get up with my seven o'clock alarm."

"What about his wife? She didn't say anything?"

"No. He made up some excuse, and she was fine with it. No one knows, and I'd like to keep it that way, sis."

"You know I'm not gonna blow up your spot, but do better."

"Ugh."

"You said twice—so what happened the second time?"

"We were in his office."

"At the church?"

"Yeah."

"You goin' to hell with gasoline drawers on. Ha!"

"Really though? It's not funny."

"No, it's not. But I don't want you to keep beating yourself up about it either."

"I'm already in hell, sis. I created this mess. And to top it all off, seeing Leah and Bekah didn't help matters any."

Taking the last bite of the flank steak on my plate, it was time for another round. I guess confessing helps my appetite because my food is gone. Ruby was so busy listening to me that I don't think she ate a single bite of the lamb she'd requested.

I start working on getting some more food. Maybe the two kinds of fish they offer will work. The salmon and swordfish are never a disappointment. The bread even starts to taste normal again for me. If Ruby and I kept going, we could end up with five servings of the bread since she told them to keep it coming.

We keep eating in heavy silence. I am lost in my own self-deprecating thoughts, and Ruby finished her food, which is nearly cold.

I sip the watery remains of my drink, wait to order another, and snag some fish and cuts of steak. Searching for the waiter to order another, Ruby gets more meat and crushes the last of the creamy mashed potatoes.

Like clockwork, the waiter appears with more sides, and I order another drink. This time, because I'm not driving, I order Henny Black on the rocks. No need to pretend that I didn't crave some liquid courage to continue speaking. Communication has never been my strong suit.

"Oh, man. I'm almost full. This food is so good!"

"The only reason I came out tonight—for real."

"So you don't enjoy my company, chick?"

"Ha. You know I do."

"I'm just playin', sis. So what happens now?"

"Other than me praying and asking why? I have no idea. I just want to go home, sis."

"You mean no dessert?"

"Maybe."

"So what happens now? What are you gonna do?"

"I seriously have no clue. Trevor is leaving anyway. Besides, I already told him we can't keep making the same mistake—no matter how good it feels."

"Was it that good, sis? I would've thought he would've been boring as fuck. Like that one dude from college. Remember?"

"Uh … which one?"

"Pick one."

"Richard was no thrill. That's for sure."

"Oh God! He was too small and too boring in bed."

"Yeah, he was. I wish you would've told me."

"You wanted to know."

"He talked a good game, but don't promise me Excalibur and give me a number two pencil."

"Ha ha! Yeah, a pencil that had been sharpened so many times, it was down to the damn eraser!"

"Girl, you ain't neva lied! Then, he went bragging like he'd accomplished something to everybody who would listen."

"Yeah, he did. He was terrible. 'Oh, baby. Oh, baby. Oh, baby. Oh, please!' I couldn't wait for him to finish and get the hell off me."

"Ruby, you're a mess!"

"What did I say? You know I'm telling the truth."

"So do you want dessert? 'Cuz I'm almost finished."

"Nah, not really. I'm barely finishing this. Why did you let me get all this food?"

"As if I could stop you."

Ruby and I eat, laugh, and reminisce about our wild times in college. Of course, she insists on paying because she is just happy to see a smile on my face. Concluding our meal and grabbing the

Jeep from the valet, Ruby takes me home. I feel better than I did before I left.

She makes me promise to call Mom, and I still feel pretty good. However, I still have the sinking feeling that nothing has really been solved. I still can't answer the question of what to do about my messy situations. The only good thing I can say is that I'd ended it with Trevor—even though I still have to deal with him because of church.

I am really tired of Shady Oak. It is kind of fulfilling to work with the youth, but I can't help feeling like there has to be something else I can be doing or should be doing. I feel like Judas standing in front of them and telling them one thing and doing another. Sometimes, I wonder what Trevor is thinking—when he isn't trying to get another shot. This will be just another skeleton to be buried once he's gone—another sinful act that I hope no one's counting. At this point in life, I've lost track.

Just as I change my clothes and get comfy in bed, a text comes in. Trevor. He asks if we can we meet at the church to discuss the youth group. If he weren't leaving, I'd just ignore it and him, but because he keeps asking me to take over, I know I have to go. Ah, dem bones, dem bones.

Chapter 10

The Hell You Say

I wake up to a muted sunrise, and the cumulus clouds seem thick with moisture. Although it's technically still winter, the birds are chirping their own songs of joy and happiness. I'd love to throw a stone at them so they go somewhere else with that nonsense. It doesn't jive well in my head this gloomy, overcast morning with promises of brightness through songs that never seem to manifest with the weather pattern. Maybe it's because I live on the East Coast. Maybe it's because it's Pennsylvania—or maybe it's because I feel like being a bitch. Yeah, I'm gonna go with option number three.

I made a promise to Ruby that I'd let Mom know I was home, which is the responsible thing to do. Do I want to? Not at all. Not because I don't think she should know, but I'm a bad liar. And once she sniffs out that something's wrong, like any mother, she's gonna press me until I tell her what happened. Honestly, I'm over the whole thing. I'd rather just move on. Mom, on the other hand, well ... not so much.

What time is it anyway? Don't these birds know that I have no reason to be up super early? It's 6:35. As if I didn't have enough trouble getting any kind of decent sleep. I'm all kinds of rest broken. I kept waking up, and I could swear I heard someone calling my name.

Yup. I didn't bring anybody home with me, so I don't know where that came from. Maybe I'm just hearing things, but I know I heard Savannah in a clear, distinctive call. Ugh. I need some coffee.

I pad my way on bare feet to the kitchen, stubbing my left big toe on my open journal. Goddamned thing! Wait. When did I take it off my dresser? Did I write something last night? Oh, well. I'll check it after I get my coffee.

Heading into the kitchen, I double-check the coffee maker to make sure I got it ready the night before. I have no clue what happens when I lack sleep, and I always have to make sure I did certain things. Thank goodness I did that right last night. Clicking the on button, I head into the bathroom to pee, wash my hands, and splash some water on my face.

This lack of continuous sleep and no clue of time has been a plague lately. I guess it's partly because it's almost time to change the clocks again. We lose an hour of sleep with daylight savings time. Not that it matters much for me anyway. I've been popping up like toast every two or so hours at night. At least according to my phone when I remember to check it.

Taking care of the bathroom business, I drag myself back into the bedroom to pick up the forgotten journal. I almost want to throw the damn thing for being in the way. There's no one to blame but me. I'd get a cat, but that would only mean a responsibility to feed it and whatnot, and I only want one in this moment just to kick it and blame it for knocking over my journal. Besides, one creature with indignant indifference in this apartment is enough.

I just want to go home.

Wow. What was on my mind last night? I'm already in my apartment. I chuck the journal further into the bedroom to make my way out. As I turn to leave, it bounces off the side of the bed and hits me square in the middle of my right foot, causing a dance with a new profanity-laced chant that I don't think even my filthy-mouthed ex would've uttered. I can't catch a break.

What's worse is that my foot is gonna bruise, and the damn journal opened to a different page. Like I feel like being bothered. My foot may fall off, but I'm supposed to write in my journal? Or even read that thing? Puh-lease! This day is already off to a shitty start. Where's my coffee? That should help right the ship.

Making a healthy mug of coffee with my favorite creamer and cane sugar is always a salve for me. Once I complete that task, I just love to inhale the smell of freshly made coffee. Ever since I was a little girl—when my grandfather would make his instant coffee in the mornings at home after he retired—I'd go down to the kitchen and find him seated with his coffee, enjoying the quiet, peaceful morning. At least until Grandmom would come downstairs, that is. Then, as I'd eat my cereal and sit quietly with Pop Pop after we'd exchanged a few words, Grandmom would inevitably come into the kitchen and clear the room because neither of us could stand when she would disturb the quiet.

I wish I had someone else to blame for the lack of quiet right now.

There's no one here but me, and I'm up way too early. I'm sure I've got those heavy, dark circles under my eyes as if I've been out all night. I can't sleep anymore. Resigned to the fact that sleep is forever lost, I take my mug of coffee and sit on the couch. It's after seven now, and there's no sun in sight. Daybreak has come, and it looks to be an overcast kind of day. Ugh. Just great.

I should probably be exercising or doing something constructive with my time, but I think I'll enjoy this cup of coffee in silence—or try to anyway. The neighbors upstairs are awake and getting their son ready for school. I can always tell because he's a little guy, and he seems to want to run everywhere. Normally, I don't get annoyed because I like kids. Not enough to have any myself, but they're cute. If Ruby ever has any, I'd love to be an auntie. Being an aunt is great because you get to play with them and have fun and show them things. Then, just when you get tired of them in your space, they get to go home. It's a win-win for everyone involved.

Picking up the remote to turn on the morning news, I find my favorite channel for this time of morning. Before seven, I like to watch channel 6. After seven, I like to watch channel 29. *Good Day Philadelphia* always lifts my spirits. I get the weather and traffic while watching the antics of my favorite morning news anchors. Because channel 6 goes national, and I still need local news and weather, 29 is the go-to channel. Plus, the folks on there get funnier as the time marches on. I guess I'd try to have as much fun as possible with the different segments too if I had to work from 4:30 a.m. until 10 a.m.

Channel 29 is still in serious news mode, so I turn down the TV and wait for the weather and traffic. Needing to check my phone for what time I'm supposed to meet Trevor, I hop off the couch and go back to the bedroom to retrieve it. Before leaving the room with my prized possession, on a whim, I pick up the offending journal from earlier and a pen. I figure I should get my thoughts in order before talking to my mother.

Like her mother before her, Mom is all about family. The only problem I have with that line of thinking is that I'm wondering how you deal with someone who is hell-bent on hurting themselves and whoever else they deem fit for destruction—even when you're related. I mean, when you're as close as Leah and I were—or as I thought we were—how do we move past this space we're in? Am I selfish for thinking that when I break up with someone that my family should too? I don't think that's an unreasonable request, I don't think that it's okay to sleep with or have a relationship with an ex of a family member. Am I insane? Am I wrong?

Once I tell her what happened, because I'm positive Leah hasn't uttered two words to anyone in the immediate family about it, Mom will probably tell me to be the bigger person and be an example as the oldest and all that other nonsense that makes no sense. Maybe that applied when we were younger and I was physically stronger than Leah, but we're not talking about having a fight over a game or Leah hiding my keys so I couldn't leave the house. We're talking about adult situations that for someone who wasn't related to me, I wouldn't be as bothered. If it was a friend who'd done that, we just wouldn't be friends anymore and I'd keep it pushing. I wouldn't see either party ever again. I'd heal and move on. But my cousin though? First cousin at that? What am I supposed to do with that?

The television has been on for at least thirty minutes, and I've missed the weather and traffic twice. I glance at the journal and pen on the glass coffee table and dismiss it with a smirk. I'd rather just focus on finding out the weather first because it may be a burn-some-electricity-all-day kind of day instead of a use-God's-light kind of day, as my grandmother would say. The sky looks like a large, tightly knitted charcoal gray quilt thick with padding. No sign of God's light in sight.

> I know you're up so I emailed a link. I think you
> might find useful. Remember nothing just happens.
> I love you, sis.

Ruby with her feel-good crap—again. She knows me too well. True to form, the email soon follows her text. Almost out of coffee and still trying to focus on the television, I opt to pee and grab another cup before opening Ruby's email. I can't really be mad since she's trying to be helpful. It's just irritating as all hell because it reminds me of something Grandmom used to say all the time: "Never let anyone be nicer to you than you are to them." Son of a ... ugh.

As it turns out, Ruby emailed me a link to a sermon on YouTube titled "Nothing Just Happens." Now, I want to be irked, but dammit, that's my sis. She knows how I feel about church and blowhard preachers. However, I can't resist the urge to click the link because I know she means well. Plus, the sermon is from one of Grandmom's favorite ministers. Gotta be honest, as someone who was raised Presbyterian, my mind wanders after the standard ten or fifteen minutes during any sermon. In that time frame, most Presbyterian ministers have finished, and the congregation is entering the response portion of the service and the time for offering.

Once I click on the link, the app opens on my phone, and I see what looks to be the ending of a choir selection as TD Jakes goes into prayer before beginning this sermon Ruby so carefully selected for me. The prayer is fine, but after he begins talking about the Bible and starts to really get into it, I'm over it. It took ten minutes before my usual annoyance sets in. That's why I don't bother with sitting in church anymore. I can't deal with the dirty looks that happen when I either pull out my phone or just leave altogether.

The last time I sat through an entire church service was around Christmas because I refused to go for Easter. One of my favorite services was the Lessons and Carols service that happens the Sunday before Christmas Eve and Christmas. It's the one where months of preparation by the choir and musicians culminate in a great service where there's no sermon—but more music and scripture readings. As one of the folks who likes singing, I always love the service because I like the singing of the hymns and anthems. And not having an actual sermon doesn't hurt. Besides, I always feel like sermons are designed to talk *at* people and not *with* them. As one who has never liked being told what to do, I never enjoyed too many sermons as a church kid. I just got used to knowing when they were about over, so I could prepare to get up with whatever choir I was on to sing during the offertory anthem. Also, most sermons are predictable. They're very formulaic. For me, that's boring. Oftentimes, it's sleep worthy, which is why I usually just stay home and sleep in my own bed. No need to nod off in those uncomfortable wooden pews that could stand a dusting. I can keep my clothes clean and stretch out as I like at home.

I will admit that Trevor has some pretty good sermons. I actually pay attention to them from beginning to end. Years ago, Shady Oak had a pastor I liked, but he gave a sermon that turned me off and showed me the hypocrisy of "Christians." I was about fifteen years old when this pastor gave a sermon preaching about the evils of homosexuality along with other things deemed evil. It was some kind of "hate the sin, love the sinner" garbage. Not only did I feel rejected because I knew I was born to marry a woman, but the message never made any sense to me. Why would God create me to hate me?

Also, why on earth would the greatest commandment be 'Love thy neighbor as thyself' if the intent isn't really to love your neighbor fully as they are? No one is perfect, but it just never made sense that hate and love could occupy the same space if God is love and we are all created in his image. Doesn't that mean we're all love too—or did I miss something? There are just too many things that don't make sense about the messages being preached by most preachers on Sunday mornings for me to ever get into church again. I'll pass on entering the building with the red doors and the big T at the top that houses hard wooden benches and stiff praises.

It's 11:11 a.m. What's a few minutes past the hour gonna hurt? At least I managed to make it here. I fell back asleep despite two cups of coffee and anger that could squeeze a bird until its eyes popped out. My mind just keeps whirling in place over the same things. Then, when some other thought trots into my psyche, I get irked all over again because I just don't like dealing with all that emotional crap. It's only because I realized that I'll have to keep stepping foot into this place until Trevor leaves.

Every time I come here, it's the same thing. Some new issue has creeped up as far as the maintenance of this creaky, old building goes. This time it's the exit sign that sits above the side doors. At first, the light had just gone out. So, if there was an emergency, you'd better know where the exit was because the sign was no help. Now, as I step gingerly beneath its exposed wires, the sign is precariously perched on one remaining screw. It appears as if the wind blows the door shut or someone slams it too hard, it'll come crashing down like the hopes and dreams of former members done dirty by heavily weighted, outworn belief systems. The only reason I'm not slamming the door is because I'm the one beneath it. Depending on who would be underneath it, I can't make any promises about when I'm standing on the other sided an out of harm's way.

Pulling open the door to the auditorium, I realize there's no tension as it slides out of my hand and careens into the wall, nearly leaving a mark from the metal knob. I lunge for the door to make sure I can close it without any additional problems. The last thing I want to do is have to pay to fix something in here. Closing the door with a gentle, yet firm grip on the knob this time, I drag my tired self to the office.

Trevor has the fire extinguisher in his hands and is looking at the copier.

"Uh … hey. Sorry I'm late. Are you okay?"

"Hell, no, I'm not okay. This damn copier was sending out sparks like it was paying homage to Memorial Day. I'm just trying to work on some things for this week's service."

"Oh, okay."

"How are you, Savannah? I'm glad you could make it."

"I'm okay. I figured I should actually come and figure out this whole youth group thing."

"Oh, yeah. Go ahead and have a seat in my office while I make sure this copy job is finished first. I know our souls are forged in the fire, but I don't think the copier sparking was what God meant."

"Ha. You mean you didn't sign up to be a volunteer firefighter too? What a shame."

"Yeah sure. Very funny, Savannah."

"Thanks. I try."

"So did you think about what I asked you?"

"I did."

"And?"

"I've been giving it a lot of thought. Too much thought perhaps. I've decided that I can't in good conscience oversee the youth group."

"What? Why not? I think you'd be great for it. They adore you."

"No, they don't. They're moody, smart-mouthed teenagers who come here for a meal and an alibi for their parents when they really wanna do something else."

"See? That's why you're a good fit. You understand them so well."

"Don't try to gas me up, Trevor. I just remember what I was like as a teenager. 'Yeah, Mom, I was at the church. There was youth group this afternoon.' The truth is I was at my girlfriend's house."

"Ha! Are you for real?"

"Uh, yeah. Don't they say whenever two or three are gathered in his name, he's in the midst or something? 'Cuz God got called on a lot while her younger brother and sister went outside to play, and her parents were at work. There were two of us. I didn't master three until much later, but I digress."

"Could you not say things like that while I'm trying to finish my coffee please?"

"My bad. Look, all I know is that I'd feel like the biggest hypocrite trying to lead these kids to the right path when I have no clue what that is beyond getting an education, finding a job, or going into the military after high school—and trying to stay out of prison."

"What's wrong with that message?"

"Nothing, I guess—except for the part where I'd have to commit to coming here at least once a week if not more. Parents would want to talk to me. So would the folks here at the church. It would just feel like it did back in the day. 'We're so glad you're working with those kids. You're one of the good ones, you know. You'll get those hooligans right!' And whatever other nonsense these people come up with that still drives me nuts."

"Savannah, I think you're doing the kids and yourself a disservice. This is and always will be your church. You belong here. They need you here."

"Trevor, I'd like to believe that's true, but you and I both know that it's not. I don't belong here."

"But—"

"Don't. Think about it. How many people in here gave you grief because of your color? Your wife's? How many fires have you had to put out because of how people treat one another in here, Trevor? How many times have you had to go to different people and ask them to stay just because someone else decided they had a little title and some prestige and acted like a jackass?"

"Too many."

"So the answer is no. I don't belong here. I never have. I can't pretend everything is okay when people start talking and acting crazy because I've experienced it one too many times."

"I hear you. I understand, but I do wish you'd change your mind—not for the church but for the youth. Who knows what will happen to them when I'm gone, Savannah?"

"I don't know. Honestly, when you leave, most of them probably won't come back anyway. To tell the truth, I'm not coming back either."

"What?"

"I'm just gonna fade away quietly. I've got some things to figure out."

"I get that."

We stop and look at each other. It's the kind of look that holds a sad knowing of things to come. He knows that I'm leaving just as he is. In the glint of amber in his brown eyes lies guilt. Guilt about abandoning the hands-on call he'd prayed for. Then, there was the other kind of guilt that we both feel in this moment. It is what angered me so early in the morning in the first place. How could I possibly be somebody's role model? My mother didn't name me Jesus. "Trevor, look ... I ... um ... about that night—"

"We don't have to say anything, Savannah."

"No, but I do. I appreciate the comfort—even though it went too far. Let's just leave it at that, okay?"

"Yeah. Sounds good."

"Okay."

"Savannah?"

"Yeah?"

"Before you go, I just want to say I'm sorry."

"Don't be. You're human like the rest of us."

"Thanks. Oh! Don't forget that I'm giving my last sermon in a couple of weeks. Will you be there?"

"Sure. Besides, my mother will probably expect me to show up anyway."

Leaving through the monkey maze that is Shady Oak, I smirk at the noonday sun. I start to walk to my car, but I pass it and make it all the way to the corner before realizing it wasn't time to go running to my favorite hideaway. I need to head over to my mother's to check on her, and I'm sure she'll bring up Trevor's leaving. The elders had their monthly meeting recently, and he gave his thirty days. Mom really likes him, so I'm set to get an earful and tons of questions that are really just rhetorical because she never likes my answers. She always gets a little pissed when I give her honest answers.

Chapter 11

Remnants of Misbelief

The time had finally come to say goodbye. Mom had harassed me to death for two weeks with the same questions in repeated fashion, all of them amounting to asking why. I'd stopped answering days ago because it wasn't about my response as much as it was just about her venting. She didn't want Trevor to know how upset she was that he was leaving—or that she was a little angry because she could see how he had grown tired of the Shady Oak way, which some people chose to perpetuate needlessly. The notorious *way* was really just folks riding roughshod over established church policies and procedures just to achieve their desired outcomes despite the needs and wants of the congregation at large.

Mom called me early this morning, despite her knowing I hate conversation before nine o'clock or coffee, whichever comes first. Typically, I preferred coffee and quiet over everything. It was a quarter to eight when my cell rang. Mom wanted to make sure I'd be in service since I'd been refusing to show up for months. Because I was a part of the fabric of the core members and came from a good family of do-gooders, I was expected to look and play the part.

The first issue was that I never could dress the way I liked. If I felt like putting on jeans, sneakers, and a T-shirt for service, the filthiness of the looks cast my way made me feel as if I needed a second shower. Then, there was the matter of speaking. In conversations, I was never one to entertain questions about my business. Church folk are the nosiest people I think I've ever met in my life. I swear if this were the Victorian era, some of the older women would want to check my underwear to see if I had unclean thoughts. If they weren't asking about what you were doing, they were trying to figure out who you were seeing. Basically, they were trying to decipher whether you were on the backslide in between Sundays.

I'll never forget how in my early twenties, a friend of my grandmother's decided to approach me, along with about two or three other women, after service where I'd been lay leader to ask about my dyed hair. I'd gone blonde because who didn't back then? If you were in the hip-hop generation that came of age in the nineties, you wanted to dye your hair blonde like Mary J. Blige or Faith Evans or Lil Kim for that matter. I was a junior in college and clubbing pretty heavily. After some nonsensical get-in-my-business questions that I didn't answer to her satisfaction, she determined that I must be some kind of wild woman who needed prayer. She kindly informed me she would keep me in her weekly prayers because, after all, it's in those dreaded college years that the youth get too worldly and forget about God and achieving righteousness or some bullshit. It's those liberal colleges that give kids ideas about pursuing various ideas freely that needed to be carefully guarded against because God forbid things change and people grow and learn. That would almost be too much.

At any rate, it took me forever to get dressed because I kept obsessing about my outfit. I knew that protocol was that I should wear a dress, but the caveat was that I wasn't going to be up front leading worship or serving Communion because it was the third Sunday in May and the sixth Sunday after Easter. I wasn't ushering, and I didn't feel compelled to wear a monkey suit and push that inner tradition button. I almost pulled out an old men's suit from what seemed like ages ago, but I changed my mind.

Once I decided on an outfit, I still took my time showering and getting dressed. Then, there was the matter of driving to the church and finding a decent parking space. Since I wasn't wearing heels, walking wasn't an issue. I was trying to remain calm enough to act like I wanted to sit through this service. I'd stayed in the car at the end of the block for fifteen minutes and debated my options. It was 10:58 a.m. If I waited a few more minutes, the service should be underway—and I could possibly avoid small talk since almost everyone would be seated. Mom told me that service had been starting later than the strict 11:00 a.m. start time. I don't even think they do the Westminster chimes anymore because they don't want to highlight the fact that they're starting late or that the organ might not work as well anymore.

***

I am thirty-three years old and scared to walk into church. How ridiculous am I? The whole thing gives me anger and anxiety and accentuates my lack of steady breathing. I've got chest palpitations. My palms are sweaty and itchy right in the middle in a tight little circle. The top of my feet have some odd pounding sensation in a small area that's causing a steady bang-bang-bang hammering rhythm to course through the veins in each foot from toe to heel. I almost had some wine this morning, but I figured that coffee was the best bet. Caffeine is not the most calming option, but smelling like alcohol at any kind of church function is never a good idea.

Maybe listening to a song will calm me down. Having a streaming music service comes in handy on Sunday mornings since most radio stations yap a lot about politics or play crap I don't wanna hear. It's 11:00, and I need about three more minutes or so before I get out of this car and head inside. Pressing play and not paying attention in my frightened state, it doesn't immediately register what's on until I hear the lyrics.

> It don't make sense, goin' to heaven with the goodie-goodies

> Dressed in white, I like black Timbs and black
> hoodies
> God'll prob'ly have me on some real strict shit
> No sleepin' all day, no gettin' my—

I quickly press pause because I'd forgotten I was listening to the Ready to Die album last night. I wanted to listen to Warning, but it turned into playing the album from beginning to this last track. Maybe that's why I wanted to wear my Timbs with my favorite pair of black jeans and a T-shirt with a zip-up hoodie. It was supposed to be in the seventies today, but it's still spring, so there's a chill lingering in the air despite the partly sunny skies. It's sixty-six degrees.

I don't feel like myself today—not that I have any idea what that means these days. The shooting pains aren't helping, but I gave my word that I'd come, so here I am. Walking. Passing the side red doors for the red sanctuary doors at the end of the block. Whoever built this church really liked red. The doors. The carpet in the sanctuary. Some of the signs inside and out. All red. Thankfully, they did replace the old sign outside the sanctuary. It is a brilliant white, which makes the lettering easier to see. Today's sermon is "Prayer: The Bridge to Salvation." Good grief! At least it was quiet from the steps. That's a good sign. The service is underway.

Once inside, I was given a bulletin and greeted by one of the ushers who kept me by the door with a disapproving stare—my outfit being the culprit—since the congregation was in the time of silent confession.

A quick glance at the bulletin let me know I hadn't waited long enough. Trevor loudly proclaimed everyone was forgiven ending the quiet. After the Gloria Patri was the Passing of the Peace. As the first notes of the hymn were playing, I made my way to a pew on the side near the back for what I hoped would be a speedy exit. Maybe if I stay in the back, people would keep it moving on the peace passing deal. There was supposed to be a particular call-and-response that I didn't care for, and it was usually when people wanted to strike up a conversation as if service wasn't underway. Nobody wants to see pictures of your grandkids—and don't ask me what I've been up to since you've seen me last, people! Peace be unto you and so on and so forth. Now, sit down and shut the hell up already!

Because of my seating arrangement, most people can't see me. Great. I've got my faux cough and peace sign ready just in case. Trevor—excuse me, Reverend Williams—is returning to the front, which is the cue for everyone to return to their seats, but not until Mom finds me. And of course, Ms. Frances is still carrying on a conversation. Loudly. It's not her fault though. She's hard of hearing now. Most of the time, what she says is hysterical because with increasing age comes a decreasing filter on appropriate speech. She's at least eighty and doesn't give a shit what you think. She's gonna say her opinion regardless of situation or volume. I remember the time she said one woman was too old to be wearing a dress that short, broadcasting business that's probably got more cobwebs than the basement of the church. I spit out my fruit punch and promptly left the auditorium and fellowship hour. Mom just looked up at the ceiling and tried not laugh. Ms. Frances had a knack for clearing the room one way or another because people started leaving with shoulders shaking and eyes cast downward with missing lips and bulging eyes full of pent-up laughter.

"Please turn to the New Testament, the book of Ephesians, chapter 1, verses 15 through 23. Listen for the Word of God:

> For this reason, ever since I heard about your faith in the Lord Jesus and your love for all God's people, I have not stopped giving thanks for you, remembering you in my prayers. I keep asking that the God of our Lord Jesus Christ, the glorious Father, may give you the Spirit of wisdom and revelation, so that you may know him better. I pray that the eyes of your heart may be enlightened in order that you may know the hope to which he has

called you, the riches of his glorious inheritance in his holy people, and his incomparably great power for us who believe. That power is the same as the mighty strength he exerted when he raised Christ from the dead and seated him at his right hand in the heavenly realms, far above all rule and authority, power and dominion, and every name that is invoked, not only in the present age but also in the one to come. And God placed all things under his feet and appointed him to be head over everything for the church, which is his body, the fullness of him who fills everything in every way.

❝ Let us bow our heads in prayer."

Reverend Williams begins to pray. I just hope I can stay focused. I totally missed the reading of the Old Testament and whatever else happened. The pain in my hands and feet has dulled to an annoying ache. Now there's this weird thing happening to my left side near my rib cage, and my head hurts. I really hope it's not one of those migraines I keep getting lately. I can't take much more of this pain, and this hard-ass pew isn't helping. What the hell is he talking about?

"By show of hands, how many of you have peace in your life?"

Oh, God. Where is he going with this?

"I see not too many of you raised your hands. So let me ask this question again. How many of you have total and absolute peace in your life? In every area of your life? Everything is just perfect. No bumps in the road at all."

Anyone who's still raising their hand is full of lies and deceit.

"I saw maybe a couple of unsure hands go halfway up and down. Notice that I never bothered to raise my hand. That's because there is no such thing as perfection people. Anyone who claims they have total peace in their life is absolutely fooling themselves. Let me explain why."

Trevor proceeds to indulge in the predictable rhetorical formula that constitutes sermons. Open with a joke or a question, which leads into a personal story that then connects to the scripture, which is broken down for the average congregant or the "unchurched" who rarely or never read the Bible, and then is connected back to the personal story and/or hook from the beginning to get the audience to think and act throughout the week—or so the pastor hopes. If there's an Eagles or Sixers game at one o'clock, then the sermon is long forgotten, and meetings are either shortened or postponed. So goes the "frozen chosen."

Somehow, I've been able to pay some attention to Trevor this morning. Maybe it's because he's chosen to discuss the drum he's been beating since he got here—interpersonal relationships—or how we treat one another. Something about us as the body of Christ's church and how, even though it hasn't been perfect, he's thankful for everyone he's met during his tenure here at Shady Oak. Blah blah blah.

My right side is beginning to hurt more. There's this piercing pain that is making me shift my weight from one side to another. It's shooting from my ribs through to my hips and down to my ankle and back up again. I can't take sitting in this hard-ass pew anymore.

It's a bright, sunny day outside of Shady Oak. Too bright. I almost wish I had sunglasses. Right now, I'd give anything to not feel this pain anymore. Rather than head to the car, I think I'll take a walk to my favorite spot nearby to clear my head. It would probably make more sense to go get some ibuprofen out of my car to help with my side, but sometimes it doesn't work. I never cared enough to figure out why.

The empty candy factory looked desolate and menacing with its dusty cameras and web-covered motion sensor lights that only gave the appearance of security. The only thing that seemed to have gotten any regular maintenance was the gate with its near pristine "No Trespassing Allowed" sign. A few feet away, there is some rotten wood, possibly from a lumber yard, for an unfinished project.

To the right, there are tiny, separate houses for empty nesters and grandparents who walk their nearly ancient dogs down this street toward the bridge that overlooks the biggest avenue that connects Philadelphia with Montgomery County.

The traffic passing beneath the bridge was minimal. My usual thinking space had already been developed by the local transit authority and their much-needed updates to its regional rail station. The bridge past the miniature homes was located next to the railroad tracks that SEPTA and Amtrak used for daily commuter trains heading to Center City or the suburbs. I like this space because I can usually sit here undisturbed by the occasional passing train—or I sometimes hop on one and see where it takes me. A lonely excursion. Always alone.

Sighing audibly, a tear slides down to my chin and wets the fabric of my black T-shirt. I start shivering, but I'm not cold. It's finally registering that I'm sobbing. Wiping my face with my sleeve, I see a singular car in the parking lot. It's probably someone waiting for a loved one. It's a Sunday morning, so it could be here in five minutes or an hour and five minutes. Who knows? Time doesn't matter anymore. Nothing seems to matter anymore.

Standing in the middle of the bridge, half of a shadow as the waves of darkness and light rested where I look at Cheltenham Avenue. Exhaling loudly, I release the piece of a tissue from the prison of my pocket and watch it float into a nearby tree. The breeze and tissue tag team wrestling a bare branch before its graceful descent toward the street.

Needing to feel something—anything—I strip out of the black hoodie. The not-quite-five-foot wall poses no problem. With its large, rounded, silver rail, I crouch facing the railroad tracks. In the distance, an eighteen-wheeler carrying bottled water and a commuter train whistle in my ears.

I've always wanted to know what it is like to fly.

Epilogue

You awake with a start. Surveying your vast surroundings, you exhale, resting in the knowledge that you are safe. You are loved, and you are well. Within the realm of eternity, there is no pain or suffering. This has never been so. You remember now.

You who have crossed the bridge into the real world can rest in the knowledge that you are free because you are love and love is freedom. Always remember to be still and know you are free.

CPSIA information can be obtained
at www.ICGtesting.com
Printed in the USA
JSHW012000020919
1250JS00001BA/2